Storm Sailing

Gary Jobson

HEARST BOOKS

Storm Sailing

Library of Congress Cataloging in Publication Data

Jobson, Gary.
 Storm sailing.

 Bibliography: p.
 Includes index.
 1. Sailing. 2. Seamanship. 3. Storms. I. Title.
VK543.J6 1983   623.88′223   83-6088
ISBN 0-87851-215-2

Contents

Illustrations by James Mitchell
Diagrams by James Sollars

*To Captain C. A. "Joe"
Prosser, Sailing Master,
U.S. Merchant Marine
Academy, for his dedicated
service to collegiate sailing in
North America.*

Acknowledgments

Many people have assisted me in putting this book together. In particular I would like to thank Marty Luray for his editorial advice and help, and Paul Larsen, publisher of Hearst Marine Books, for his patience while the material was being gathered and written. Also Adlard Coles, whose fine book *Heavy Weather Sailing* helped inspire this volume. And others, who gave unstintingly of information and ideas—Chris Bouzaid, Don Cohan, Dick Curry, Arnie Gay, Anne Hayes, Courteney Jenkins, Gary Lucier, John Martin, John Mecray, Sam Merrick, Jeff Neuberth, Kevin O'Connell, Charles Oman, Capt. Joe Prosser, Lynn Rader, Wally Ross, Hal Roth, David Slikkers, Geoff Stagg, Peter Stalkus, Rod Stephens, Donald Street, Robert Symonette, Ted Turner and Dan Wellehan, Jr. Thanks too to the editors of *Sail* magazine and to the Offshore Racing Council, the Southern Ocean Racing Conference, and the United States Yacht Racing Union, for general help and permission to excerpt from their publications.

It is with gratitude that I recall the opportunities I have had to sail on many of the world's finest ocean racing yachts, where I gained the experience to write this book. To their owners, my appreciation—especially Bob Bell (*Condor*), Warren Brown (*War Baby*), George Coumantaros (*Boomerang*), Walter Cronkite (*Wyntje*), George Eddy (*Windance*), Herbert von Karajan (*Helisara VI*), Huey Long (*Ondine*), Jan Pehrsson (*Midnight Sun*), Ted Turner (*Tenacious, Courageous*), Bill Whitehouse-Vaux (*Mistress Quickly*), and Arthur Wullschleger (*Golliwogg, Fire One*). And also to the Barnegat Bay Yacht Racing Association, the Chesapeake Bay Yacht Racing Association, the Middle Atlantic Intercollegiate Sailing Association, the Texas International Sailing Association (*Ranger*), the New York Maritime College, the U.S. Merchant Marine Academy, the U.S. Naval Academy, and the members of the *Defender/Courageous* Group.

Gary Jobson
Annapolis, 1983

Storm Sailing

All sailors have their own views on heavy weather sailing. Most have wondered, perhaps even when day-sailing in stronger than normal winds, how they would cope with the "ultimate" storm. Offshore cruising folk beginning a lengthy ocean passage know that eventually they and their boat are going to be tested by gale force conditions. It takes preparation to deal with 25–35-knot winds and even more knowledge and experience to deal with 65+ storms, and that is what this book is all about—to offer the experience learned over many years of sailing and racing, to help the skipper and his crew face the perversities of wind and waves, survive, and keep sailing.

Heavy weather sailing is the cutting edge of the sport. When the wind comes up and the sailboat comes alive, one reef is taken, then two, and sails are reduced to the smallest the boat can carry and still maintain speed under control. At times like this, concentration on trim and boat-handling is absolutely essential. Beyond that, handling hour after hour of high winds and heavy seas is the final test of crews, gear, and, indeed, the boats themselves. The problems faced by the weekend skipper in dealing with a fast-moving, violent line squall,

Introduction

and by the racing skipper trying to survive in the midst of the 1979 Fastnet Race, are, after all, only a matter of degree. The lessons applied to the first are to a much greater extent applicable to the second, and that is what this book is also about—to make the connection between the two.

When telling heavy weather tales, novice sailors tend to exaggerate wind velocity. I often hear young college sailors talk about the 25-knot breezes in which they've raced, and I figure that the breezes probably averaged 14–17 knots. New offshore sailors have described to me how heavy the weather was at night, but I remember that generally waves look bigger and the wind seems stronger during the night hours. There are unusual noises, violent motion (often from bad steering), spray coming on board, and personal uncertainty causing the beginning crewman to fear heavy wind.

As the wind increases, survival conditions vary with the size of the boat. In a moderate-size cruising boat, with one or more seasick crew members, the need for survival techniques begins at Force 7 (28 to 30 knots and sometimes less). For most boats, Force 8 (35 to 40) is the most the boat can stand and still sail. Boats of 40 feet and less have difficulty sailing when the wind is consistently blowing more than 40 knots.

My own experience with heavy weather began while growing up on Barnegat Bay on the New Jersey shore. Hurricanes, although potentially devastating, were a special time for us. We lived close to the water and the Beachwood Yacht Club, so it fell to my father, brother, and me to secure the boats in advance of a storm. In 1954, during Hurricane Hazel, all the dinghies at the yacht club were lugged 150 feet up a hill and set on their dollies around our house.

At that early age I learned not to fear heavy weather, and in fact I thrived on those days when the wind was up. At New York Maritime College it of course never seemed rough enough for our 500-foot training vessel *Empire State IV*. Although I found I was prone to sea-

sickness like many other sailors, in time I learned how to overcome that as well. And I found through the years that heavy weather conditions often bring out the best in both skipper and crew.

Still, there are times when even the best heavy weather sailors can't handle it—especially in small boats. Prudence dictates returning to shore. In January 1980 I was racing a 21-footer in the Frostbite Series off Annapolis, Maryland. I had two strong Naval Academy midshipmen crewing for me, but the breeze became so strong that we could no longer sail the boat safely. On that blustery Frostbite Sunday the boat kept spinning out violently. No matter how hard we tried, the crew could not handle the boat. I simply told them it was time to take the sails down and head back to the dock.

Gary's mother Helen Jobson, the author, and brother James sit on a Barnegat Bay Sneakbox, one of a number of club dinghies that survived Hurricane Hazel in 1954 after being hauled to their house near the bay.
Thomas Jobson

Introduction **3**

To sail or not to sail is a question that only experience can answer; you'll find some thinking about these choices in the pages of this book.

One of the ways of making these choices is by listening to weather forecasts before you go out. But even this lacks accuracy and the sailor may be put on his mettle despite all precautions. Storms can come up quickly as they do on Chesapeake Bay near my home, or on the Jersey shore where I learned how to sail.

I'll never forget a freak squall that caught 200 boats off guard sailing near Little Egg Harbor on the Jersey coast. The squall came up without warning and when the weather cleared 15 minutes later 90 percent of the boats had capsized in some part of the bay. I remember in that Little Egg Harbor storm watching E-Scows sailing at 20 knots, planing across the mud flats right up into the marshes, the race committee having set the finish line about a hundred yards from the shore. Under the squall conditions the boats couldn't stop once they had crossed the finish line.

Sailors have survived hurricanes and even used the cyclonic winds on the fringes of the storm to speed them on their way. They have survived pitchpoling and 360-degree capsizes offshore while their boats were dismasted and the interiors virtually destroyed. But with the hulls still afloat they created jury rigs that brought them to safety. The stories are legend; Miles Smeeton and his wife Beryl survived two such disasters in South Atlantic storms as did the racing yacht *Doubloon* off Cape Hatteras, North Carolina.

Hull design and construction, rig detail and strength, and crew ability are the keys to storm survival, and that is why I pay attention in this book to the 1979 Fastnet Race in great detail. The lessons of Fastnet cannot be avoided by anyone interested in storm sailing. In fact, it was my experience aboard Ted Turner's winning *Tenacious* in that race that led me to write this book.

Probably no race has been rougher than the 1979 Fastnet in which 15 sailors were lost at sea and 77 boats did not finish. Some were sunk; others were abandoned or reduced to hulks. After our rounding Fastnet Rock and getting intermittent weather forecasts that the wind would be Force 8 to 9, perhaps 10 to 11 locally, it started to dawn on me just how heavy those winds might be. They didn't disappoint us, blowing 60 to 65 knots for a good deal of the night with waves building to at least 35 to 40 feet. I spent seven incredible hours at the helm of *Tenacious* that rough night. I can remember wondering to myself, as I crouched behind the wheel wearing two safety harnesses, how anyone could accurately describe the storm. There is no pictorial record of how rough it was that night.

Yet, not once did I ever fear for the boat, myself, or the rest of the members of my watch. At 0330 the crew was forced to shorten down to a #4 jib and no mainsail at all. It was almost impossible to walk about the deck and yet 17 members of the crew were able to wrestle the main off the boom. Then daylight came and we were able to get a storm trysail flying.

The lesson of sailing with an experienced crew is an important one. Had more crews during the 1979 Fastnet sailed in heavy weather before, perhaps the tragedy would have been lessened or avoided. The Race had been a holiday for many sailors. When the storm occurred, much of the fleet was simply unprepared. *Tenacious* was not. Ted Turner believes in having the strongest and best equipment available and in the Fastnet storm his attitude paid off. *Tenacious* had no major equipment breakdown and crew morale was high, probably because the crew was so experienced. Many members were veterans of America's Cup and major offshore races around the world. The fact that we had competed two days earlier at Cowes Week in 45-knot gusts made everyone more comfortable with the heavy weather of the Fastnet storm.

But Fastnet was the test. The 630-mile race has been run every year since 1925 except during the Second World War. The course begins at the Royal Yacht

Squadron at Cowes on the Solent, goes out along the south coast of England and across the Irish Sea, then around the Scilly Islands to the finish in Plymouth, England.

Having made it through the night of the storm, we headed home with two jibs set wing and wing—a #1 to leeward and a #2 to windward. Using a storm trysail we could sail straight downwind with the trysail acting as a weather vane of sorts. When it filled on one tack, we steered in the opposite direction to keep the boat moving downwind. The waves were awesome. The stern would rise up so high you felt you'd be catapulted over the bow, but at the last moment the boat would wildly start surfing down the face of the wave with spray spewing out from either side of the bow.

As we approached the Scillies the wind began at last to lighten. Even at that moment we were unaware of the tragedies that had occurred around us during the night. We had heard scattered radio messages, but it wasn't until we reached the dock at Plymouth that we realized the extent of the disaster. There were hundreds of people waiting for word on boats and crews. The crew of *Tenacious* was in a festive mood as we came into Plymouth because we felt we had won the Fastnet on corrected time, but the mood left us when we realized what a sad event the race had become. In the end, of the 303 boats that had started, only 86 finished. Four yachts under 35 feet sank. Worst of all, 15 lives were lost.

The debate surrounding the 1979 Fastnet still continues. Many race committees, however, now strongly enforce safety regulations and measurement rules as a result of the Fastnet disaster. One area that has never been adequately discussed is what happens to a crew during a storm as it goes from racing to surviving to completely giving up hope. What causes a sailor to give up?

I suspect that experience is the key to overcoming this sort of crew failure. Rotating watches, attempting not to get seasick, keeping warm, dry, and comfortable when offwatch—all help you think clearly and therefore sail better even in the worst of conditions. Having a boat that doesn't react violently to wave action is also very important. Violent action on the hull fatigues a crew, and when sailors get tired they no longer think clearly. That is when serious errors are made. Just one experienced crew member encouraging the rest of the crew during a serious storm will make everyone feel more comfortable.

Chris Bouzaid, an experienced offshore sailor who was a member of the 1979 Fastnet fleet aboard the Australian racer *Police Car*, points out that safety and speed go hand in hand. As long as the boat is moving, crew morale is high and therefore the boat is safe.

But there is more to it than that. The idea is to sail through storm conditions with a confident attitude that you will not only survive, but enjoy it. It is my hope this book will show you how.

TO RACE OR NOT TO RACE

There is a point when, because of worsening weather conditions, it is no longer practical to sail or race hard. The strains on hull and rigging become so great that when the boat is pushed, the vessel and crew are in jeopardy. The crew can no longer handle the boat. The question for the skipper is how to recognize when to stop racing safely and start worrying about survival.

In a dinghy, the great fear in stormy weather is capsizing. But there are times when capsizing is better than sailing out of control toward a rocky shore. You should

be prepared for coping with a capsize, and, in fact, test yourself on the recovery of boat and crew in calm weather so you have a routine to follow. A self-righting dinghy may be better off capsized because the overturned hull is easily spotted. But stay with the boat and make sure that in your preparations you have equipped the crew with life-vests (USCG approved) and that the crew members are wearing them. And be certain that everything that can float away is tied down.

On larger boats at sea, it is often easier to ride out a squall or a storm than risk sailing to a harbor. Many ships have tried to beat a storm in and have ended up

CHAPTER 1

Racing vs. Survival

on the rocks because the storm got there before the vessel made it to safety. Inability to maneuver, heavy surf in narrow inlets, reduced visibility, and unfamiliarity with aids to navigation may all dictate staying well out to sea until it blows over.

Running for shelter during a sailboat race is something that does not often happen. As truly heavy weather infrequently occurs while racing, many sailors are not aware of just how rough it can get. And for that reason, storms during regattas make the events even more memorable. But unfortunately, dropping out has somehow become unthinkable. John Rousmaniere, who participated in the 1979 Fastnet aboard an American entry, *Toscana,* wrote in his book *Fastnet Force 10:* "Longer foreknowledge of the approaching low probably would not have decreased the havoc caused by the storm. We on *Toscana* had come too far to drop out of this Fastnet Race because of a few warnings about bad weather. Of the two dozen or so boats in the Fastnet that lost men overboard, suffered incapacitating damage, or were abandoned by their crews, perhaps one or two but no more might have run for shelter if the Force 10 warning had been made during the BBC radio shipping bulletin early on Monday morning."

This sort of attitude is relatively recent. Less than 30 years ago, offshore racers shortened sail at night for fear of the unknown. Perhaps weather forecasts were unreliable or crews were not experienced enough to handle nocturnal emergencies, but yachts would change to smaller headsails or take a tuck or two in the main to avoid sailing out of control. Shortening sails made for better sleeping, but the yacht slowed down.

On the first night of the 1981 Marion (Massachusetts) to Bermuda Race on *Wyntje,* skipper Walter Cronkite and the rest of the crew informed me that it had been decided to shorten sail. We had received a forecast for thunderstorms in the area and the crew said they would feel more comfortable with less sail up as we stood watches with only three to a watch. Perhaps 25 years of racing has made me less than conservative so I objected to the decision, but was outvoted seven to one. We switched from a large #1 genoa to a working jib. Had a storm hit we would have been in good shape, considering how shorthanded we were. But there were no storms and all we accomplished was a reduction in speed.

Nevertheless, whether you have a crew that likes to push or you have a crew that races more conservatively, it pays to be prepared. I anticipate wind changes constantly. During my watch I always prepare for the next two possible sail changes, deciding whether we will need a larger, fuller jib, or a smaller, flatter one. I keep a new jib sheet or spinnaker sheet lead handy and stow the next sail to be used just under the sail locker hatch, ready to be handed up.

How hard to push is a question of attitude. When yachts are moving fast, as mentioned, crew morale is high and the crew naturally performs better. It's much like driving in a car. The most frustrating time in traffic is when there is constant starting and stopping. When the car moves along at a constant pace, the spirits of the driver and the passengers brighten.

Similar to shortening sail at night, another old racing habit was to heave to or lie ahull in gales. The 1949 Wolf Rock Race off the English coast was, according to Adlard Coles, the first time small ocean racers carried on through most of a storm. After that race, lying ahull or using a sea anchor was no longer part of the racing scene.

Expert opinions vary on when to stop racing or sailing. U.S. Olympic Yachting Committee Chairman Sam Merrick says "it is time to stop racing when you begin to break equipment." For designer Rod Stephens, a veteran offshore racer, "the critical point between racing and survival is between 50 to 55 knots of wind." Racing and cruising yachtsman Wally Ross advises "stop racing when life or pocketbook is in danger."

For me the key in races is to try to keep racing longer than your competitors. It is challenging to test the limit of your boat, your equipment, your sails, and yourself. As long as you are thinking clearly and can accept the risks involved, sailing hard will help you get more experience. Certainly anyone who goes to sea must accept the risks. Still, my racing aim must of course be tempered with the goal to minimize any unnecessary danger.

During one race in heavy weather, our boat's mast seemed to be bending more than most of us felt it should. The owner stated simply, "Well, now we'll be able to see if this rig is good or not." When the boat was dismasted a short time later, the owner surprised us all by saying "It's the best thing that could have happened. It's better to break down now by the beach, than when we're offshore on the way to Bermuda."

The more you put the boat to a test, the more confidence you will have in it. Check equipment before you leave to make sure everything will function smoothly. Every yacht that goes to sea should have a detailed list of equipment to check before sailing. Not all breakage can be predicted; metal fatigue, for instance, can't be detected without x-ray analysis. Knowing that the job has been done, however, will give you more impetus to push just a little bit more in heavier weather.

Some Sailing Tips:

• Check the wind. If a storm builds gradually, it is often difficult to tell how hard the wind is actually blowing. On a broad reach, for example, an experienced crew on a strong boat will move along easily and steadily—despite the wind being as much as 35 knots, and perhaps increasing.

Sailing in a building storm, I look around often to see how bad things are becoming. A reliable technique is to luff the boat into the wind to see exactly how wind conditions are. When you are running it is especially difficult to judge the wind; at ten knots your apparent wind is less than when you are heading into it at five.

• Slow down if you need to. Most sailors assume that the competition is continuing on at full speed when they slow down. My own experience has been that when my boat slows down because of heavy weather, or we take precautions like dousing the spinnaker, the competition probably is still carrying on—but with great difficulty. They may well end up far behind.

Such an incident happened during a Block Island Race. Returning from Block Island to Larchmont, New York, a strong easterly gale came up. Our C&C 39 had spun out at least ten times before we doused the spinnaker and went to a double head rig—two jibs set wing and wing, the one to windward on a spinnaker pole. We watched a competitor accelerate and leave us astern; he was still under spinnaker and broached periodically.

"Be prepared so you can take what comes, even though you hope to be lucky."

Racing vs Survival **13**

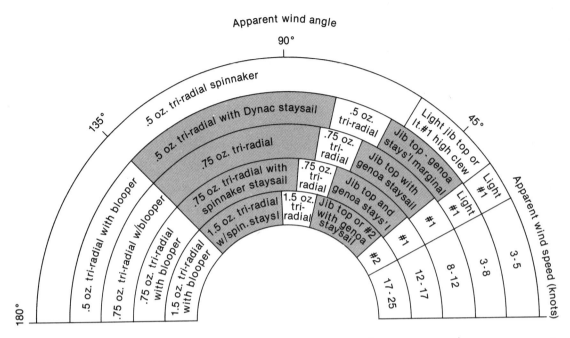

Apparent wind angle

90°

135°

45°

.5 oz. tri-radial spinnaker

.5 oz. tri-radial with Dynac staysail

.5 oz. tri-radial

.75 oz. tri-radial

.75 oz. tri-radial with spinnaker staysail

.75 oz. tri-radial

.75 oz. tri-radial

1.5 oz. tri-radial w/spin.staysl

1.5 oz. tri-radial

Light jib top or genoa

lt.#1 high clew

Jib top with stays'l marginal

Jib top with genoa staysail

Jib top and genoa stays'l

Jib top or #2 with genoa staysail

Light #1

Light #1

Light #1

#1

#1

#2

3-5

3-8

8-12

12-17

17-25

180°

.5 oz. tri-radial with blooper

.75 oz. tri-radial w/blooper

.75 oz. tri-radial with blooper

1.5 oz. tri-radial with blooper

Apparent wind speed (knots)

Figure 1: *Develop a chart for your boat similar to the one above that shows the correct sail for every wind condition and wind angle. (Courtesy Shore Sailmakers)*

When the sun came up the next morning our competitor was nowhere to be found. After finishing the race we saw him limp into the harbor hours later. He had blown out all his spinnakers and halyards and made port under jury rig. The old saying "haste makes waste" was never more true.

• Know your boat and the proper sail combination and steering angle for every wind condition. Make a chart (see diagram, page 14) based on your own experience and the thoughts of the boat's designer and sailmaker, to determine what sail is right for what wind condition. Make a practice always to use the right sail at the right time.

RACE MANAGEMENT

The ultimate decision to race or to abandon because of heavy weather rests solely with the skipper of a competing yacht. It behooves race committees, therefore, to make sure that races are held under the most favorable conditions. Rescue boats should be available for any emergencies. The race committee not only runs the races, but it should also insist that competing yachts carry proper equipment and sails. The race committee can also screen the competitors and rule out the inexperienced, as is the custom in such regattas as the Kennedy Cup at the Naval Academy in Annapolis, the Cruising Club of America's Newport-Bermuda Race, and now the Fastnet.

The United States Yacht Racing Union publishes a manual outlining the specific responsibilities of a race committee. In addition, USYRU issues a set of regulations stipulating the specific equipment that must be on board, depending upon the race. In its own booklet, the Southern Ocean Racing Conference describes the responsibility of the skipper toward his crew very clearly:

"A complete and accurate list of names and addresses of the crew on board must be filed with the race committee at the skipper's meeting." (The list should also contain the telephone number and contact of each crew member should there be a problem during the race.)

"The safety of the yacht and its crew is the sole and inescapable responsibility of the skipper, who must ensure that the yacht is fully found, thoroughly seaworthy and manned by an experienced crew who are physically fit."

The skipper of the yacht must be satisfied with the soundness of hull, spars, rigging, sails, and all gear. He must ensure that all equipment is properly maintained and stowed. A stowage plan should be posted in an obvious place on the boat, showing the location of each piece of equipment. Every crew member should know where flares and safety equipment are stowed so they can be obtained quickly and without hesitation when they are most needed. Equipment and rigging should be checked at least once a year by experts. Before a major ocean passage, it may be worth having rod rigging and spars x-rayed for cracks and metal fatigue.

SORC rules are specific about a skipper's overall duties and responsibilities:

16 Storm Sailing

"Neither the establishment of equipment regulations nor any inspection of a yacht in any way limits or reduces the complete and unlimited responsibility of a yacht's skipper. . . .

"It shall be the sole and exclusive responsibility of the skipper and crew of a yacht to decide whether or not to continue a race. . . ."

ABANDONMENT

The decision to abandon a race must be made with great care, since it can create considerable confusion amongst the fleet of boats; their skippers are concentrating on racing and not on signals from the committee boat. In some cases, races can be abandoned before they are started. The New York Yacht Club's America's Cup Committee, for instance, will not start a race if the wind blows continually at 25 knots or more for three consecutive minutes.

In the 1930s, when a group of big boats including the giant J's and other larger yachts raced on the south coasts of England and Ireland, the race committees carried a special torch. If the wind blew out the torch it was ruled too windy to race.

It is, however, almost the nature of the sport for races to be sailed in all conditions, light and heavy, much like a football game that continues regardless of wind, temperature, snow, or rain. This is most true of offshore races; it is next to impossible to abandon an offshore race once it starts. The Fastnet Race Committee in 1979 was highly criticized in many press reports for not cancelling the race when the storm was imminent.

An investigating committee, however, could not recommend any policy that would place on race organizers a duty traditionally assigned to the master of every seagoing vessel. There was also no provision for calling off a race once it had started. In any case, abandonment would have been impossible. The fleet was spread over

In small-boat sailing (opposite page), when the boat becomes too difficult to handle because of increasing wind and seas, it may be time to head for shore. The decision rests with the skipper.
Carol Singer

Racing vs Survival **17**

hundreds of miles of ocean to and from Fastnet Rock. It was emphasized by Alan Green, secretary of the Royal Ocean Racing Club, that the safety of a boat and its crew is the sole responsibility of the owner or skipper.

Criticism of the Fastnet Committee was nevertheless rampant, particularly regarding the lack of provisions for dealing with potential disaster. Skipper and owner Dick Nye, in an article in *Yachting* (March 1980), said: "You have an attractive nuisance. The Fastnet Committee is promoting a race which they are encouraging people to enter. To say there should be no special coverage for these yachts that have been encouraged to come by promoting the glamor of the Fastnet Race . . . is wrong. The race committee is totally abrogating (its) responsibility."

Chris Bouzaid was aboard the Australian entry *Police Car,* which survived to finish first in its class. He wrote: "It's like running in the Indianapolis 500 and having no fire-fighting equipment . . . it is the race committee's responsibility to prepare itself . . . handle something going wrong."

Another example of the abandonment question came from Dick Nye, who pointed out that in 1968 a hurricane had come up the East Coast between Bermuda and the mainland. It was forecast and the Newport-Bermuda race was postponed for one day. Had the hurricane arrived a day later it might have hit the fleet. This happened again in 1982 when the CCA committee postponed the start for two days due to hurricane force winds in the Gulf Stream.

The question is, what could the Bermuda Race officials have done if the fleet had been hit by the storm halfway to Bermuda? The answer is, nothing. In the case of the 1979 Fastnet, unprepared though officials were at the start to cope with trouble, rescue efforts after the fact were impressive primarily because of the training and indefatigability of the British Navy and other rescue teams. One hundred thirty-six sailors were plucked off yachts and life rafts during the storm. Although crew inexperience, boat size, and lack of proper equipment have been credited with causing most of the losses, it has also been pointed out (*Sail,* May 1982) that the experience level of the skippers was high and there seemed to be no significant difference between damage and knockdown suffered by boats of the least experienced skippers and the most.

Still, the lessons of Fastnet were not lost. Significant changes in RORC Special Regulations and requirements for the Fastnet Race should have universal repercussions. One of these concerns experience:

"In order to be considered for acceptance as a starter, the RORC will normally require the skipper and at least half the crew to have competed, in the yacht in which they are intending to race, and in the last twelve months preceding the Fastnet start, in either two RORC races, one RORC race plus another 200-mile race, one RORC race plus a 300-mile non-stop passage, or to present other acceptable evidence of experience of a similar kind."

The result has been the shrinking of the Fastnet fleet, down 31 boats from the 303 that sailed in 1979 to 274 in 1981. Abandonment did not have to be considered

On the morning after the 1979 Fastnet storm Jim Mattingly is at the helm of Tenacious *as she heads for the finish line at Plymouth. Seas are an estimated 25 feet, the wind 50 knots.*
Greg Shires
Brad Sullivan

for the next Fastnet Races, but remains a controversial issue. Changes in the RORC requirements were also very important.

They include: "Every boat must carry a storm trysail; a toerail of not less than 25 mm must be permanently fitted around the deck forward of the mast. Every boat must have a bow fairlead, closed or closable, suitable for attaching a towing or anchor warp. There must be at least two manually operated bilge pumps, one operable from above deck and the other from below. Each pump must have its own discharge pipe and may not discharge in the cockpit unless the cockpit opens aft to the sea. Bilge pumps must not be connected to cockpit drains. Bilge pump handles must have a lanyard or catch or similar device to prevent accidental loss. Life rafts must be carried on deck, or in a special stowage opening immediately to the open decks. Each raft must be capable of being got to the lifelines within 15 seconds. At least one horseshoe-type life ring must have a pole and a flag and the pole must be permanently extended and attached to the ring with 25 feet of floating line. The flag must fly at least six feet off the water."

In 1981, RORC rules also stated that every entry had to be fitted with a marine radio transmitter.

My own conclusions concerning abandonment are that in offshore racing it is the responsibility of the skipper and crew to handle their own yacht.

In dinghy racing or closed-course one-design sailing, however, it is up to the race committee to decide on abandonment. In this case careful observation of how a closed-course fleet is handling the weather is the key. Should more boats be in danger of capsizing than can be adequately handled by the committee the race should be cancelled. There should be a provision in the sailing instructions clarifying what skippers should do if a race is cancelled, or if a boat drops out.

In offshore racing, the SORC has been particularly stringent in its rules regarding a boat that has abandoned a race. Rule 13 says:

"A yacht which has abandoned a race should wear her ensign and keep well clear of yachts racing. The skipper must, at the earliest possible opportunity, notify the race committee and the USCG of this fact. Failure to give such notification will result in disqualification, and at the discretion of the SORC rejection of entries for future races."

Local regattas do not have such stringent rules, and problems invariably occur in locating competitors who have dropped out. Should a competitor go ashore during a squall, he should get to a telephone quickly to notify regatta officials or the sponsoring club that the crew is safe.

In the spring of 1970 as a third classman at the New York Maritime College, a friend and I went sailing on a windy day in March. Our boat was a Skipjack, a small

In their first meeting, the author (sail no. 21) crosses Ted Turner (24) as they race in 30-knot winds in Marshall 15s, during the 1972 North American Interclass Solo Championships on Narragansett Bay, R.I.
Ray Medley

"A police boat came along, put a line around our mast and towed us to shore."

dinghy. We planed back and forth across the entrance to the East River and found ourselves on the leeward shore close to the Throgs Neck Bridge in Queens, where we capsized. The water was cold and we spent most of the time clinging to the bottom of the overturned boat. Luckily a New York City police boat came along and put a line around our mast and towed us to shore. A helicopter came to assist in the rescue although it wasn't necessary.

We pulled the boat up on the beach, and a police car very obligingly drove us back to the Maritime College through rush hour traffic where we were surprised to find our coach and team members very concerned. We should have called in as soon as we reached shore. Unfortunately, we had spent an hour in a traffic jam while others were worrying about our fate. The lesson was a good one.

The 1977 Championship of Champions Regatta hosted by the U.S. Naval Academy in Annapolis is another good example of both missing crews and the question of abandonment in closed-course races.

A fleet of 23 boats started the first race in mild 10- to 12-knot winds. However, a squall hit on the last windward leg and the winds reached 30 knots and gusted higher. One competitor whose boat was turtled estimated gusts at over 60. There were a number of crash boats on the scene to assist the sailboats, but because of the heavy seas and cold water, several crews were taken off their boats before it was possible to right them and take them in tow. The boats were anchored and towed in later when the storm subsided. Other racers were forced onto the beach at nearby Tolly Point and returned to the Naval Academy by car.

Unfortunately, darkness fell before it was possible to know the whereabouts of all of the crews, and two Coast Guard boats were called in to join the search. It was many hours before all sailors were accounted for. No one was lost or injured, but those who had made it to shore should have called in at first chance to avoid widening the search.

Incidentally, the race committee was blamed for trying to finish the race despite the impending storm. They had gambled unsuccessfully on finishing because the racers were on the last leg.

Although no closed-course race committee enjoys making the decision to cancel a race while the boats are on the last leg, safety is a paramount consideration. This is particularly true when juniors are racing or when the boats are not self rescuing. I spent many years racing Penguin dinghies. They sail well until they capsize and can not be righted. Some clubs that race Penguins and other boats like them have crash boats with high-speed pumps to get the water out and the boat on its feet again. A better approach would be to design a self-rescuing Penguin. Anyone that sails in the winter in frost-bite regattas should be sailing in a self-rescuing boat, and it is essential for clubs to consider this in their schedules.

RESCUE MANAGEMENT

When I coached at the U.S. Merchant Marine Academy we had a rule that no race was ever started without at least a race committee boat and two backup Whalers on the water at all times. If both Whalers were occupied with rescue, the race committee kept a special watch for other capsizes. If one more boat capsized, the fleet was sent back to the beach. My rule was to have one crash boat on the water for every five dinghies racing. A fleet of 20, therefore, required a committee boat and three Whalers to patrol the course.

Each crash boat had at least two people on board—one to drive and the other to throw lines. Among the equipment each boat carried were large bailing buckets, a high-speed motorized pump, a VHF radio, a hand pump, and a line with a life jacket attached to it for people in the water to grasp. To get enough bailing buckets we raided local laundromats for Clorox bottles, which make satisfactory bailers when the bottoms are cut off. One enterprising raider returned with 400, enough for a two-year supply.

Some General Rules:

• If the water is cold it is essential to rescue crews as quickly as possible to avoid hypothermia (abnormally low body temperature; see Appendix C).

• Competitors should wear life jackets on the water at all times. Most racing associations require this. (Middle Atlantic Intercollegiate Sailing Association rules stipulate that any competitor not wearing a life jacket is automatically disqualified.)

• By using a loudhailer to give instructions, rescuers can be very helpful to the crew of a boat that has capsized. First, make sure that none of the capsized crew is injured. Speak in encouraging tones, and give the crew specific jobs to do one at a time.

1. "Lower the sail." When that task is completed,

2. "Let's right the boat," perhaps by using the jib sheet over the gunwale to bring the boat up. Then say,

3. "We'll take your painter and pull you around into the wind."

With this step-by-step approach, the capsized boat can be righted quickly and calmly.

• Some race committee crash boats have difficulty handling a capsized dinghy, particularly if a mast goes into the muddy bottom. In this case the only solution is for the crash boat to anchor directly upwind of the capsized boat, and get the crew to release the stays and the shrouds so that the mast comes loose. Then place a life preserver or buoy to mark the mast, right the boat, and tow boat and mast to the beach.

• The Race Committee should see that storm warnings are hoisted on the club flagpole. At the Academy we used the red small craft advisory pennant to recall a fleet. If the watch on duty, the sailing master, or the coach received a forecast for storms or heavy winds, the red flag was hoisted on the end of the pier and the fleet was required to return to the basin.

• Crash boats should be in radio communication with each other, if possible, while operators keep a watchful eye on the fleet.

• The worst move a race official can make is to go in the water to try and rescue a capsized yacht or its crew. The Red Cross rule of thumb is "throw, row, or go." In other words, throw a line, go after a victim from a boat, and, lastly, go into the water. It is dangerous to leave the crash boat and far better to bring the capsized crew into the rescue vessel.

SAILING TO WINDWARD

Sailing on the wind in heavy air is the essence of the sport. The seas are big. The boat works hard as it pounds into the waves. This duel with wind and spray is an ancient battle—as old as the history of seafaring. Rail down, the rigging throbs and the helmsman is challenged to keep the boat on course and moving. Everything is trimmed just right, the boat is well-balanced, and when you arrive at your destination or return to the harbor you feel you've achieved the true sailor's goal—the ability to handle your boat under adverse conditions.

It's not an easy task. In heavy weather, mistakes are costly. Whipping blocks, loose sheets, stiff sails that don't come down in a hurry, small things that go wrong are multiplied by the force of the wind and the plunging seas. Therefore, every move must be deliberate and planned in advance. Harnesses must be used. Falling overboard is a distinct possibility although every sailor believes that it won't happen to him. Injuries range from minor to incapacitating and can come very suddenly.

Sailing on *Tenacious* at night once in a rough Gulf Stream blow, I was forward changing a sheet from one headsail to another when the boat hit an abnormally big

CHAPTER 2

Heavy Weather Sailing Techniques

wave. Three feet of green water washed down the deck, lifting me up and carrying me down the deck with it. I grabbed for every object I passed and finally hung up on a cockpit winch with my legs half overboard. The boat came upright and I climbed back, then ran forward to finish changing sheets. It wasn't until moments later that I realized how dangerously close I had come to being lost overboard. My safety harness went on and stayed on until the storm eased.

Another weird but not atypical accident took place on the maxi-racer *Ondine* in 1978, while we were practicing reach-to-reach jibes in San Francisco Bay in a strong breeze. I stood in the vicinity of the mainsheet while directing traffic, paying no attention to where my feet were placed on the deck. On one jibe, the boom swung across with great force, and unknowingly I put my foot into a loop of the mainsheet. Without warning I found myself picked off the deck, feet above my head, and dragged across the deck with my elbows hitting every piece of gear that wasn't flush with the deck. It was a painful lesson.

Injuries are more common during heavy weather because it is much harder to keep your balance. Sailing a 25-foot sloop in a 40-knot storm not long ago, we prepared carefully for a jibe, but one crewmember slipped in the middle of the maneuver and put his hand on the traveler as it swung from one side of the boat to the other. His hand was trapped as the traveler car hit the side of the cockpit. The result was a broken bone and a curtailment of sailing as his hand healed in a cast for six weeks. As careful as we were, we should also have secured the traveler car in the middle of the track; most travelers have double lines or a spring-loaded pin for this purpose.

As the wind builds, so do the seas. The need to "de-power" the boat becomes essential. Going to windward in heavy weather, the biggest error is allowing the boat to heel too much, creating great difficulties in sailing. Cavitation occurs when the boat is at an extreme angle and air gets trapped between the keel and the bottom of the boat, forcing the boat to make leeway. A boat that is heeling too much is out of balance and difficult to steer and is receiving unnecessary strain on its rig and headsails.

When the apparent wind is between 25 and 40 degrees off the bow, the angle of heel is critical. For narrow boats, a 35-degree angle of heel is acceptable; for wider and lighter boats, up to 25 degrees is the maximum. Try to keep the boat well balanced, with no more than five degrees of weather helm. When the heel becomes too great de-power by using the traveler, or reduce sail to keep the boat on its feet. The tendency as the breeze comes up is to overtrim sails when going to windward. But boats are easier to handle with the sheets eased several inches. The tacking angle is wider and the boat becomes easier to steer. When you are heeling more than you need to, the rudder begins to act as a brake, slowing the boat down and creating a harsh weather helm.

When the boat is sailing in balance, crew members are comfortable—particularly novice sailors who are unsure of themselves to begin with. When the rig is not functioning properly, the boat is overheeled, there is excessive weather helm, or the boat is not being sailed at a consistent angle of heel, the crew becomes uncomfortable. They seem to sense that the boat has taken control. Never allow this to happen. Keep speed up.

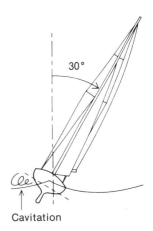

Figure 2: Excessive healing of 30 degrees or more creates cavitation between hull and keel, which in turn causes leeway.

Preparation

Prepare for windward sailing in heavy weather by testing your sails in advance. On a calmer day, set the storm trysail and storm jib. Where do the reef points go? Mark their position on the main boom. Try all the smaller jibs.

Then, on a day when the wind is blowing more than 15 knots, make a date with your sailmaker so he can critique your sails and advise you on their trim. The shape of the sails is critical. Heavy weather sails should not be cut too flat. A fine leading edge is not forgiving because it creates excessive sideways thrust and no forward drive. Flat sails unbalance the boat and make it difficult to steer.

De-powering Techniques

As you begin sailing in heavy air you'll learn some of the techniques used to de-power the sails. The standard goal is to flatten the sails and open the leeches.

First, flatten the mainsail to the point where the outhaul is all the way at the outboard end of the boom. By trimming the mainsheet you move the draft aft. You can return the draft forward by tightening down the Cunningham.

Trim the jib halyard to get all the wrinkles out of the sail. When you find that you're overpowered, move the jib lead aft and ease the sheet to spill wind from the top of the sail. This is called twist and it reduces the heeling moment because only the bottom halves of the main and jib are now working.

Since the luff of the mainsail is built in a curve, the sail can be flattened by bending the mast to correspond to the curve. On a small boat, a boom vang or the judicious use of the mainsheet will do it. When the mast bends excessively, a ripple will appear from the clew of the sail to the maximum point where the mast is bent, usually about 60 percent of the way to the top.

Use of the Boom Vang

A boom vang can be an effective tool on the wind in heavy air. In existence for at least a half century, the vang is also known by other names—boom jack, kicking strap, and boom downhaul. In the early days of yachting, crew members sat on the boom to keep it from bouncing from wave action. Generally a vang is a strong block-and-tackle arrangement with one end attached to

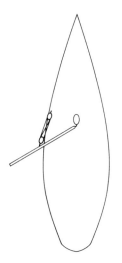

Figure 3: *A boom vang can be used as a preventer or foreguy if it is attached to the boom as close to a right angle as possible.*

the boom roughly a quarter of the way aft from the gooseneck, and the other end attached to the base of the mast with a swivel block.

The boom vang helps the boat sail faster by keeping the boom under control. It gives the sail better shape and prevents the boom from riding up and down in choppy seas and spilling air out of the main. The vang also helps stabilize the roll of the boat. But it should not be confused with a preventer, which is a line from boom to toerail used when a boat is running before the wind, to secure the boom against swinging inboard during an unscheduled jibe or violent roll.

The vang can act as a traveler. When the mainsail is eased the boom will ride up unless a vang restricts it. When the vang is tight and the main eased, the boom will not ride up and spill wind. In smaller boats, this technique is called "vang sheeting" and has proven to be very fast.

The concept of vang sheeting in windward sailing was popularized in the mid 1970s. Art and Joan Ellis won the Fireball World Championship with Art (190 pounds) on the wire and Joan steering by using the vang-sheeting technique. Instead of feathering the boat on every puff, they simply eased the mainsheet but kept the boom vang tight. When they got a puff, instead of feathering into it, they bore away from it and had the boat planing. Although they lost several degrees of windward distance by doing this, the tremendous boat speed they gained put them well ahead of the fleet.

Aboard this pocket cruiser, the boom vang is used as an accidental preventer.
Martin Luray

A vang can help on other points of sail too. When the wind is aft of the beam, the vang helps to create more sail area. By keeping the leech of the sail tight you make the sail take better shape. The maximum amount of draft is where it should be, in the middle of the sail. As a rule, you can tell how well strapped down the vang is by looking up past the boom to the topmost sail batten. The batten should be parallel to the boom.

In heavy-weather windward sailing there are other ways to de-power the force in your sails than by flatten-

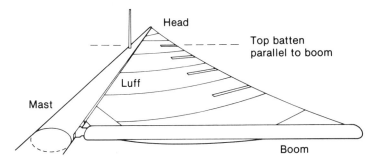

Head

Top batten
parallel to boom

Luff

Mast

Boom

ing the main and opening the leeches. Having your crew weight to windward further helps keep the boat from heeling too much.

The Australian 18-foot skiffs deal with the problem nicely by sailing with a rack extending five and a half feet from the hull to get the crew weight placed right. When the wind builds, weight should be moved aft. Weight forward causes the bow to bury itself in the seas.

Teamwork while racing aboard the yacht Gaboon. *The crew not in action sits on the windward rail while tactician (aft) and helmsman pair off. The only other person in the cockpit is the trimmer.*
Carol Singer

Mast Rake

Raking the mast aft reduces the height of the sail plan and also reduces heeling force. It has the same effect as moving jib leads aft. Mast rake is controlled by a headstay, a backstay, a pre-bend in the shrouds, and perhaps by a baby stay—a stay running from the middle of the foredeck to the middle of the mast.

These Australian 18s have rigs for every wind condition. Masts range from 27 feet for storm conditions to 38 feet for light air.
Dan Nerney

Although it is advantageous to be able to rake the mast forward and aft, sidestays should be kept tight so there is little give in the system. This helps keep the jib luff straight and gives the boat more power. But problems can arise with a rig that is too tight.

On the maxi-yacht *Condor* in 1981, for instance, we tightened the rig by using a crowbar on the leeward shroud to the point where the top of the mast was slowly twisted out of column. The result was a very costly dismasting.

During the 1980 America's Cup trials aboard *Courageous,* we had been sailing with shrouds that we tightened each day. Racing against another contender, *Clip-*

per, with a stiff breeze of 30 knots over the deck, we were using a Kevlar mainsail with no give in it and a new hydraulic boom vang, also with no give in it. As we worked to windward, something had to give. Finally a tang at the spreaders let loose and the mast toppled over the side.

There has to be some give in the system. The easiest and most effective way of dealing with it should be having a mast that bends, or else rapidly trimming and easing the mainsheet. If a mast is too straight or the main luffs continually, lee helm will develop.

Use of the Traveler

Playing the traveler in heavy weather can be a tremendous help to the helmsman because the helm is a good gauge of the boat's balance. In rough water, the maximum rudder angle should be five degrees; any more creates leeway and the boat becomes unbalanced. (Helm is determined by the mast position, amount of heel, sail shape, and the disposition of crew weight.)

One way of judging helm is by reference marks in the cockpit for the tiller, or on the steering wheel. When the boat is out of the water, turn the rudder and mark off rudder positions in one-degree increments. Start with the rudder amidships, and move it to port and then to starboard. Using a large protractor you'll find that each degree of rudder movement corresponds to several inches of tiller or wheel movement. For the tiller, use tape to make marks on the cockpit sole or deck. For the wheel, use tape or marline on the wheel rim, to mark off the angles.

Once you have the references and are racing in heavier air, the mainsail trimmer can easily see the amount of helm you're contending with and adjust the traveler accordingly. If the main trimmer sees that there is more than five degrees of weather helm, the traveler is moved to leeward. If the traveler cannot move any further to leeward and the helm is still more than five degrees,

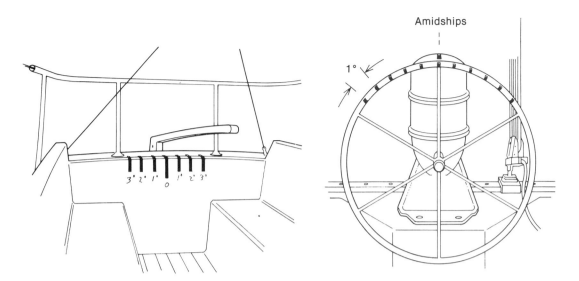

then the mainsail should be eased and perhaps the traveler moved back amidships. It is references like these that help a crew work as a team and keep occupied during heavy weather sailing.

Figure 5: *Reference marks on transom and wheel allow you to adjust helm against sail trim and compensate angle of heel.*

Backstay Tension and Sheeting

Heavy air genoas are most efficient with a maximum of backstay tension. In heavy seas, however, with a #3 genoa, ease the backstay tension to 85 to 90 percent of maximum to reduce the shock loading. When sailing with the heavy #1, you usually cannot trim the halyard and sheets tight enough. The opposite is true for the smaller #3 and #4 genoas; the jib lead of these sails should be inboard to keep the sheeting angle between 7 and 11 degrees. It may be necessary to use a barberhauler to bring the clew of the jib inboard, but be careful not to overtrim the jib and create too fine an entry, because the boat will become difficult to steer.

Reefing and Setting Up Sails

Reefing is still a prime choice for the cruising man dealing with heavy weather. Racing sailors generally have more options. It's possible, for instance, to stay with a full main, but set a full hoist jib that is very short on the foot. The boat stays at speed, especially when it drops into wave troughs. Under normal seas, but windier conditions, the use of a non-overlapping jib keeps the slot open and the boat also functions at speed.

The recurrent question is whether it is better to reef the mainsail or go to a smaller jib. The answer varies with the boat, the sails available, and the wind and sea conditions. One method used by racing sailors is to develop a graph for every apparent wind angle and wind velocity, then test different sail combinations under those conditions when they occur. Note which combinations keep the boat at speed yet still comfortably balanced. Normally this is done by comparing your performance with boats in the vicinity on the same tack.

Try to keep luffing to a minimum, because it puts much stress on the sails. Sew battens into the mainsail tightly so they won't work their way out of the batten pockets. Don't let leech lines fly; they'll get hung up when you tack, and rip the leech. Sails should be made with pockets for stowing the leech lines.

When setting sails, keep the leech lines eased until the desired shape is reached. Once you have determined the amount and position of draft, then take up tension on the leech line to eliminate flutter. Remember not to overtrim; an overtight leech will distort the sail and make it inefficient. However, flutter is as bad as an overtight leech. A flapping sail breaks down its fabric and wears out quickly. It is also inefficient, because the airflow is broken up before it can be effective. (See Figure 6).

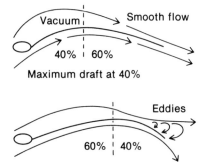

Figure 6: *In heavy winds, the draft in a sail tends to move aft in causing leech to be too tight. Keep the draft forward for more speed and maximum sail efficiency.*

Dealing with the Wind

Wind shifts in direction and velocity occur as often in heavy air as they do in light air, but changes in the wind are often harder to detect. I have not yet found wind in any body of water in the world that does not have holes in it. They are caused by small thermals on the water, boats that have passed through the wind, or simply contours in the flow of the breeze. It's the responsibility of the helmsman to watch for approaching puffs, and to decide whether to feather up or ease the traveler. Concentrate on maintaining the angle of heel that keeps the boat going fastest.

Dealing with the Sea

Keep in mind that sea conditions may differ on opposite tacks. On one tack with the seas on the beam, it might be useful to carry more sail so that the boat can point higher. On the opposite tack the boat may be heading into the seas, in which case the sails might be sheeted further outward with more twist, and not trimmed quite so hard, so that the boat will keep up speed.

The biggest error in trying to keep up boat speed is overcanvasing. With proper sails for the conditions, drive as low as ten degrees off course so you can power through the seas. Experiment until speed, sail trim, and crew condition look and feel "right." The emphasis is on speed and balance, not super pointing ability.

REACHING

Reaching is a very stable point of sailing, and when you're on it you should do everything you can to make the boat feel alive. It is also the fastest and safest point of sail in heavy weather. The boat is sailing closer to the wind than on a downwind course, so there is little threat of a jibe. The waves approach generally from the beam or slightly on the bow.

Balance is again the key to performance during a heavy weather reach. The best sail combination is a small high-clew headsail, and a staysail underneath, creating a double slot effect between headsail and main. When the apparent wind is between 45 and 80 degrees, jib overlap doesn't help performance. Excessive overlap tends to create sideways motion without much forward motion.

A double head rig, on the other hand, keeps the center of effort low and develops a considerable amount of power when reaching. Adjust the leads so that there is some twist in the jib. When the sails luff they should be backwinded at the head of the sail first.

On a reach in heavy weather, water over the deck or in the headsail is also a problem; that is another reason for using a high-clewed headsail. If reaching with a #3, which is not high-clewed, it is worth taking a topping lift, attaching it to a grommet added along the foot of the headsail, and lifting it several feet so that water no longer runs into the sail. During the Fastnet storm, my greatest fear was the clew of our #4 ripping out because of the weight of water coming aboard.

If the main boom touches the water on a reach, take a flattening reef, or else the first reef. Watch the knotmeter, and if the speed goes up when the main luffs it is time to reef down. If the boat goes out of control, the fastest solution is to ease the boom vang so that the mainsail luffs and the boat can be steered away from the wind. Keep an eye out to windward watching the water for heavy puffs. If you see one approaching, anticipate by sailing a lower course and have the sail trimmer stand by to ease the sails.

Steering on a Reach

Helmsmen wear out quickly on a heavy weather reach and should be rotated often. When racing, I believe 15 to 30 minutes is the maximum someone can steer effectively on a power reach.

Some steering tips:
• Keep your neck and face clear when reaching, so you have a better feel of what the wind is doing.
• Pick a point ahead to steer by. This can be another boat, a cloud, or a star, but you need a reference point other than the waves on the horizon.

• Allow for five to seven degrees of leeway when steering on a reach. The faster the speed, the straighter the course will be over the bottom. Rapid adjustments to sail trim will help keep you on your course.

Reaching with a Spinnaker

Sail trimmers have as much to do with controlling the boat as the helmsman when racing in heavy conditions. Examples are legion.

During the 1979 Cowes Week while racing downwind on *Tenacious,* we had *Williwaw* close at hand under the command of America's Cup skipper Dennis Conner. A huge gust swept in from behind. A number of boats wiped out behind us, many with their spinnakers overtrimmed. Several spinnakers simply blew out, ripped to shreds by the 50-knot gusts. Included was the spinnaker on *Tenacious.*

Conner avoided the same fate for *Williwaw* by easing the spinnaker out as the puff hit. The trick was to keep the spinnaker pole exactly in position and also to keep the clews of the spinnaker separated, so there was no chance of the chute wrapping around the headstay, or of the pole hitting the headstay, or of the sail rubbing against the spreaders or rigging. His boat's speed may have dropped one or two knots, but Conner never lost control of the boat and continued on course with his sail intact.

There are times when it is simply not possible to fly the spinnaker any longer under reaching conditions. On the 51-foot sloop *Midnight Sun* during a heavy-air Miami-Nassau race we held a slight boat-for-boat lead ahead of *Williwaw* and 21 other competitors. We had crossed the Gulf Stream under spinnaker, but as we came closer to Stirrup Rock the wind went ahead. Only one of our helmsmen could keep the boat on course without broaching. When others tried, *Midnight Sun* broached every few minutes and lost valuable time to the competitors around us. Had we been smarter we would have doused the spinnaker on the second broach, set a double head rig, and made our course while losing little distance or perhaps even gaining on our competitors.

The heavy weather spinnaker should be small and carry very little overlap. Its shoulders should be flat; it might collapse sooner than a normal chute, but this is important in keeping the boat under control. The small spinnaker can be used with either a staysail or a #4 headsail underneath for a double slot effect.

Keep the spinnaker pole away from the headstay by at least one foot. Crew members should be aware that when the pole height is lowered, the pole moves closer to the headstay. So when an ease in the topping lift is called for, the guy trimmer should be ready to trim the pole aft. Crew members should also stand by, ready to ease staysail and main sheets the second that the helmsman feels he is losing control of the boat. The pole should be trimmed so it is at an angle perpendicular to the wind. A piece of yarn acting as a telltale in the middle of the pole will help adjust these positions.

When apparent wind direction is from 100 degrees to 150 degrees, the wind is pushing the boat and no longer pulling it. On this angle of sail the spinnaker must be free in the leeches. A barberhauler can be used on the spinnaker sheet to play the chute. In lighter puffs, trimming the sheet forward tightens the leech. In heavier gusts, ease the barberhauler off to free the leeches. In light air we want power. As the breeze comes up we want to de-power.

Staysail Trim and Dealing with Heeling

There is a myth that it is helpful to overtrim a staysail because that pulls the bow away from the wind. Myth it is; any sail with a tight leech forces the boat *closer* to the wind. The only solution is to luff the sail. As the boat sails into a gust, ease the sheets. When the boat is at full speed, tracking nicely with a balanced helm, trim the sails back in.

As in windward sailing, concentrate on angle of heel. If the boat heels too much ease the sails. If there is too much weather helm ease the main or reduce backstay tension to move the mast forward.

Be sure the staysail does not interfere with the wind from the spinnaker. Watch the instruments carefully. If the staysail is luffed and the speed increases, it's time to take it down.

Riding the Waves

Finally, even though most reaching is done with the waves abeam, it is possible to ride them to get maximum speed. On *Boomerang* in the 1982 SORC, helmsman Jim Whitmore caught a wave on a beam reach and got the boat surfing at a speed of 19.5 knots—that speed is the all-time record in more than a thousand miles of SORC racing.

You can use the seas to advantage by riding the waves and keeping the boat on course. In dinghy racing on a power reach, the experienced racer sails above the course of other boats to get free of their chop, and to take advantage of the fact that waves are stronger and more consistent to windward of the line of boats.

When reaching with a dinghy, maintain control by getting the centerboard about halfway up—to de-power heeling forces and also to ease the boom vang. Attention to sail trim and good steering will ultimately get you distance in the "passing lane."

DOWNWIND SAILING

There is a British saying, perhaps apocryphal, that "gentlemen don't go to windward." If this is true, then downwind sailing is the reward for all those ungentlemanly nautical miles spent bashing to weather—slogging it out in head seas and contrary winds. Sailing off the wind, "sailing free," is the *pièce de résistance* of the sport—the dessert after a meal of spindrift, sloshing water on deck, and breaking wave tops. Off the wind, sheets are eased, foresails boomed out. Foul weather gear comes off, the wind hits the back of the neck instead of full face, the seas break over a stern quarter giving the boat that extra feeling of having a life of its own as it dips and slides across the waves and into the troughs. Whether racing under spinnaker, or cruising the trade wind belts under twin headsails, downwind sailing can be delightful.

Then, when heavy weather comes the crew has the option of dousing the spinnaker or watching it tear itself to pieces. Steering becomes a chore—the epitome of challenge and concentration for even the best helmsman. In big seas, downwind sailing implies the possibility of broaching and/or taking a knockdown. But it should not be feared. For cruising sailors or racing skippers, downwind sailing under control is a matter of technique and experience.

If there is a wild side to cruising, it is running before the wind in towering seas under sunny skies dimpled with trade wind clouds. For me, as a racer, the finest hours of the sport have always been that final downwind leg of the Miami-Nassau Race—sweeping into Nassau under spinnaker, the rest of the fleet like so many lollipops on the horizon.

Spinnakers in Heavy Weather

For racing as opposed to cruising, flying a spinnaker in a heavy breeze is customary. But it takes good crewing and experience to stay out of trouble while going for the tremendous amount of speed that can be generated while sailing off the wind. Going downwind, the spinnaker can actually stabilize the boat and make steering easier. The trick is to maintain boat speed and sail a comfortable course. Sailing directly downwind is not easy; the boat is always on the edge of jibing or broaching because it is in an unstable condition, but there are ways of dealing with this that become routine through experience.

To Set or Not to Set, and How

In winds under 30 knots, a normal spinnaker can be used. In heavier weather, about 30–35 knots of wind, a storm spinnaker is more practical if a spinnaker is used at all. The typical storm chute is smaller with narrow shoulders and is made of 1.5-ounce nylon spinnaker cloth.

As boat size enlarges, spinnaker material must be sturdier. On boats of 50 feet or more, storm spinnaker cloth will weigh 2.2 ounces, while on the maxi cruising and racing boats it can weigh as much as three ounces. Anything heavier than that becomes unsafe, strangely enough. The force of the wind against the tight weave of the heavier cloth could blow out the rig. Better to have the chute tear than to lose a mast.

You can carry a full mainsail and a spinnaker comfortably in 30-knot winds with the apparent wind at 150 to 180 degrees. And bear in mind that having the spinnaker over on the windward side of the boat is equivalent to having four times the main on the leeward side.

When setting the spinnaker in heavy breezes, several rules apply:

To prevent the chute from wrapping, be careful not to trim it aft more than 45 degrees and to separate the clews as much as possible with at least a third of the sail on the leeward side of the boat. Do not fill the sail until the halyard is at the top of the mast. Control problems develop when the spinnaker gets off to one side of the boat, and it is at this point that the boat takes over and the helmsman is no longer in charge.

On modern IOR yachts with high-aspect-ratio rigs, a blooper set to leeward of the spinnaker will help balance

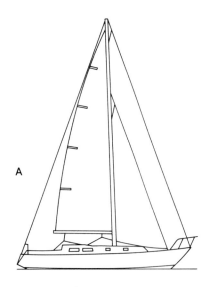

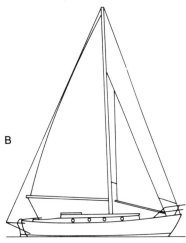

Figure 7: *Racer/cruiser (A) has high aspect main and jibheaded rig as opposed to classic cruiser (B) with low aspect main, which is long on the boom, and fractional club-footed jib.*

the boat because the center of effort will move back to the middle of the boat again. With a blooper, the spinnaker pole can be trimmed back to almost 90 degrees of the centerline. The spinnaker sheet is eased until the leeward clew is trimmed to the headstay. (See boats in Figure 7.)

Since 1978, IOR boats have been built with deeper, more powerful rudders to give the helmsman better control. The trend toward smaller rudders had started in 1967 with the Twelve-Meter *Intrepid;* in 1970 both *Intrepid* and *Valiant* had tiny rudders, and these Twelves were difficult to steer. Ocean racers followed suit, but sanity has prevailed on ocean yachts and Twelve-Meters for the last several years.

Sailing by the Lee

When the wind hits your sails over the leeward quarter while sailing downwind, you are sailing by the lee. It can be advantageous in heavy air if handled delicately because the technique cuts down on dangerous time-consuming jibes. Keeping up speed is essential in sailing by the lee; when the boat slows down it is in danger of getting out of control and broaching or going through an uncontrolled jibe.

In this form of downwind sailing, the boat's destiny is in the hands of the helmsman. Watch the masthead fly often. Avoid sailing more than 20 degrees by the lee. If the boat feels out of control, luff up to regain balance.

To maintain boat speed, the helmsman should steer the boat to leeward in a puff and reach up to gain speed as the puff goes by. The helmsman can also surf down the waves, using them for acceleration. The technique takes concentration and a feel for the seas. Watch for the deepest trough and head the bow into it, steering the boat at a 90-degree angle to the waves. Just before the wave passes under the hull, accelerate by trimming sails, heading up and keeping the boat on an even keel with no pressure on the rudder.

Maintaining Boat Balance

The key to downwind sailing in heavy air is keeping the boat balanced and under control. Move crew weight to windward and aft, and avoid crew forward of the mast. Proper balance dictates about a five- to ten-degree windward heel.

Another way to steady the boat is to "choke" the spinnaker by overtrimming it—keeping equal tension on both sheet and guy and ensuring that the clews are on opposite sides of the headstay. When both clews are on the same side of the boat, rolling and instability will be invited. Overtrimming, however, can also cause an unscheduled jibe; guard against this by rigging a boom vang as a preventer from midpoint on the boom to the leeward rail.

Broaching

Broaching in heavy air most often occurs when the spinnaker is on one side of the boat, as when reaching. The vessel, driven by a quartering sea, begins a bow oscillation when the helmsman loses control. The spinnaker may dip into the water, making recovery even more difficult.

Heading up may forestall an approaching broach, but when it does happen, recovery seems to take forever. The trick is to get the air out of the spinnaker as fast as possible. Ease the sheet (not the guy), or, in an emergency, let it run. You can also loosen the spinnaker halyard, but it is best to ease one control at a time. In any case, once the pressure on the spinnaker is eased, the boat will right itself.

In heavy seas, however, when the boat takes a knockdown there is danger of water rushing into the companionway and flooding the interior. For this reason, the companionway hatch should be kept closed. In fact, the Cruising Club of America requires for the Bermuda Race that yachts keep companionway hatches covered and secured to deck level. Several boats in the 1979

Some broaches can be prevented. When the boat becomes unstable, the quick solution is to sail 20 degrees higher, release boom vang to get the boom out of the water and the boat back on its feet.
Sharon Green

The cardinal sin in an impending broach is letting the foreguy go so that the pole rides up the headstay.
Sharon Green

This boat is about to lose it. To get out of this crisis, release the spinnaker sheet.
Sharon Green

And this boat has lost it. To get back up, ease the vang, tighten up on the pole and let the spinnaker sheet go. In heavy seas, make sure the hatches are all closed.
Sharon Green

Heavy Weather Sailing Techniques   **47**

Fastnet Race had companionway hatch covers and wash boards that simply dropped off when the boats broached. Since that race, the rules have been changed; the companionway hatch cover must either be locked in place or be a permanent installation.

When easing sheets in an endeavor to bring the boat upright, remember to keep the foreguy, topping lift, and afterguy trimmed tight to keep the pole under control and away from the headstay. In fact, easing the foreguy is extremely dangerous under those conditions. If the pole goes up the mast (held only by the topping lift) it will most certainly break off at its mast fitting and will be completely beyond control.

Getting the Spinnaker Down

If the weather becomes too heavy for a spinnaker, a jib rigged to windward will guarantee almost equal speed. Set a spinnaker pole to windward with the windward jib sheet passing through the jaws at the outboard end. Use the pole topping lift and the foreguy to position the pole before the jib is brought across. Slowly ease the jib across with the new windward sheet taut to avoid wrapping the jib around the headstay. A leeward jib can also be set. Cruising boats can use another spinnaker pole for this wing-and-wing rig. Long distance cruising boats, expecting to follow the trade winds, can reduce chase on sails, and ease steering with a special two-pole downwind rig, sometimes called simply "twins." When racing, however, the rules permit the use of only one pole.

In dousing the chute, a staysail hanked to the intermediate forestay will help blanket the spinnaker and make the takedown easier. It also helps to "hide" the spinnaker behind the windshadow of the mainsail. Cruising skippers can use a "sleeve" to control the spinnaker when setting or dousing it. Working properly, the sleeve "swallows" the voluminous sail and captures it into a roll that is easily dealt with on deck.

JIBING

Experienced crews can jibe a spinnaker in almost any conditions, but inexperienced skippers and crew must calculate their moves in heavy conditions much more in advance. One technique is to hoist the headsail, drop the spinnaker, jibe, then reset the spinnaker. The method is slow but effective.

Another technique is the two-pole jibe. A new spinnaker pole is set before the mainsail is shifted over, and a second set of guys and sheets is clipped into the spinnaker and the new pole before the boat is jibed. Now when the spinnaker is jibed it remains under control.

Jibing a small planing dinghy in heavy air takes practice and some courage, because to be accomplished under control it must be done at high speed. Get the boat planing as fast as possible while sailing directly downwind, and snap the mainsail across, making sure that the sheet is clear and won't be fouled on any object as it swings across.

The S-jibe is a technique for keeping a dinghy under control during a heavy-air jibe (see pages 50-1). Start the S-jibe by bearing off. Keep the boat sailing by the lee. Now, overtrim the main (pull it in). As the mainsail swings across, steer back in the main's direction. This move changes course, reduces the power in the sails, and doesn't allow the boat to round up into the wind. As the main fills on the new side, keep it overtrimmed and resume your new course, having completed the jibe. Don't begin to head up until the boat is under control.

Some jibing tips for dinghies:

• Keep the boat flat. When you start to jibe, change course as little as possible. Once a boat starts rounding up, it is very difficult to stop, particularly when the end of the boom is dragging in the water.

• Be careful not to ease the sheets out too far. Never allow the main to ease beyond perpendicular to the centerline of the boat, as would be possible with an unstayed mast.

• Change hands, switching the main sheet and the hiking stick (or tiller) before the boom swings across, so you are in your new position immediately after the jibe is made.

TACKING

Tacking in heavy air requires thorough preparation and good crew coordination. Be sure that the jib sheets are clear to run. If there is a second safety sheet, remove it. The main sheet traveler should be anchored on the centerline so that it doesn't slam wildly down its track when the boat comes about.

Coming about should be done when the boat is sailing at full speed. Bear off five degrees to get the boat up

to speed, then tack rapidly to avoid pounding and stopping, especially in big seas. As soon as the sails fill on the new side, let the traveler out to leeward to relieve the helm and keep the boat from being forced up into the wind. Once the tack is made, a backup sheet can be secured to the windward clew, and sail trim adjusted to deal with the requirements of sea conditions and wind angle.

In a dinghy, be sure that cam cleats are set at the right angle and the sheets can be freed instantly. One major cause of capsize in heavy weather is a sheet being hung up in a cam cleat as the boat comes about. Where cleats are used, a half-hitch that can be removed quickly is all that should be used to hold a sheet.

You may find tacking impossible and decide to wear as an alternative. Wearing is a technique of bearing off

The S-jibe is used to help de-power the force of the wind on the main and keep the boat sailing. In this dinghy technique, as you get by the lee, turn back in the direction the main was going.
Christopher Cunningham

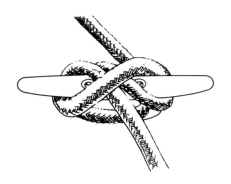

Figure 8: Cleating a sheet with a half hitch allows you to release the line quickly.

and jibing and then coming up on the wind—almost like a U-turn in the water. If you do use this technique, keep the traveler anchored on the centerline and make sure the crew is aware of the maneuver. The main will be let off as the boat comes off the wind, then sheeted in hard for the jibe.

STEERING

No matter what maneuvers are contemplated, whether racing or cruising, the helmsman is the most important person on the boat. The boat must maintain course, stay up to speed, counter sea conditions, and not be in danger of broaching; it is up to the helmsman to see to all this. Steering in storm conditions is challenging and fatiguing, and requires that the person at the helm be totally clearheaded and have no other job except steering.

As the wind flows across the sails, the boat responds in a complex pattern of changing loads. The stresses placed on the boat are magnified both by the fickleness of the wind as it changes direction and by the confusion of the sea. Through this conflux of air, water, and boat and their sometimes erratic interactions, a helmsman is expected to guide several tons of offshore yacht. If you sail a dinghy, quick response is even more critical, as the weight of just one wave is far greater than a dinghy.

There are several ways to do it; fewer ways to do it well. What steering requires is the recognition that all sailboats have an optimum range between pinching and footing, that within this range the boat will sail upwind in a combination of maximum speed and maximum pointing. Generally, the faster the boat, the greater the range. While a catamaran might have an optimum steering range of as much as five degrees, a Twelve-Meter may have a groove of no more than one degree and the modern IOR yacht about three degrees—certainly small margins on which to concentrate.

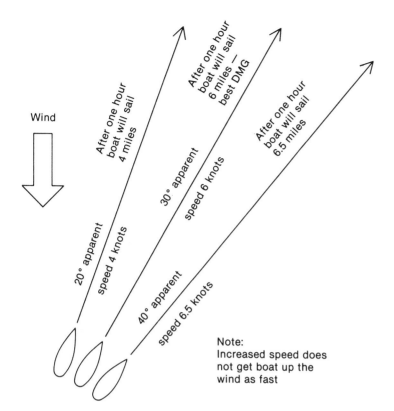

Wind

After one hour boat will sail 4 miles

20° apparent
speed 4 knots

30° apparent
speed 6 knots

After one hour boat will sail 6 miles — best DMG

40° apparent
speed 6.5 knots

After one hour boat will sail 6.5 miles

Note:
Increased speed does
not get boat up the
wind as fast

Figure 9: *In heavy weather find a course that is the most comfortable and efficient for your boat. The diagram shows the possible range available going to weather, with the boat sailing at 30 degrees to the apparent wind, which is the most optimum course.*

To steer precisely through such a narrow groove, the helmsman must use every source of information available—the waves, angle of heel of the boat, wind on the water, apparent wind direction and strength, the masthead fly, and all instruments in the cockpit. Most important for racers, of course, is the boat's performance relative to other boats. Competition is the best benchmark for judging speed and heading.

Telltales other than the masthead fly should be relied upon only sparingly, because they are distracting. The masthead fly is much more important as the wind shows changes at the top of the mast first—a good indication of lifts and headers. Most masthead flies have an angle index which can help you judge the boat's apparent wind angle. If as you sail to windward your apparent wind is generally 30 degrees to a tack, spread the mast-

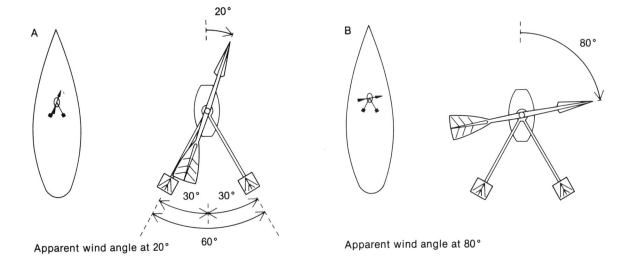

A

20°

30° 30°

60°

Apparent wind angle at 20°

B

80°

Apparent wind angle at 80°

Figure 10: *The masthead fly is a useful guide to keeping course when on the wind (A). The vanes are spread to 30 degrees, the arrow shows a 20-degree angle off the apparent wind; the combination shows that the boat is too close to the wind for efficient sailing. On a reaching course (B), because the vane is atop the mast, it will tell wind direction before lower telltales do.*

head fly angle indicator to 60 degrees so that the arrow will be directly in line with the appropriate indicator when you are hard on the wind.

When sailing a course, you naturally use your compass for reference. But don't be compass-bound—pick a point on your heading to steer to. It can be landmark, a navigation aid, a cloud, or another boat. If it is moving, of course, check your compass frequently and find an updated reference mark.

When a yacht sails upwind it must overcome several obstacles, none more harmful than waves. To overcome their effect steer as if the bow is an extension of yourself and with as little tiller or wheel movement as possible. If you can, aim the boat so that the waves push the boat slightly to windward. At the very least, avoid intersecting them on anything less than a 45-degree angle. Remember that it is better to foot the boat too much than to steer too high and slow.

Another obstacle for the person at the wheel is weather helm, which is tiring for the helmsman and slows down the boat. The rudder in effect acts as a brake, because it is used to counter the pressure on the main that causes the boat to heel. To counter weather helm, move the crew to windward or shorten sail. You can also ease the traveler, ease the sheets, rake the mast forward, or flatten the main. The headsail and mainsail trimmers must coordinate with the helmsman to ensure that the boat is performing at top efficiency. The main can be flattened or made fuller, the draft moved forward or aft, and the genoa coordinated through sheet tension or by changing the draft with headstay tension to suit wind and wave changes.

The trimmers can help attain an optimum angle of heel through sheeting and sail handling, which will also neutralize weather helm and rudder drag. While most boats are designed to pick up waterline length and, theoretically, speed as they heel, remember that too much heel can make the underwater foils less efficient, causing the boat to make more leeway. Since your compass course is actually higher because you are forced to steer the boat into the wind to compensate for the boat being overpowered, excessive heel is sometimes difficult to recognize. Your course made good, though, will show that you are losing ground.

Steering is often a combination of details that make the difference between winning and losing. Such seldom-considered items as posture and clothing (you must stay warm and dry) can influence the outcome of a race. Stand to windward as you steer so you can see the sails working together and can concentrate on the angle of heel. Keep yourself in a position that allows you to see everything around you, and exert as little energy as possible to keep that position, so you can go the distance.

Going the distance may be as much as an hour or as little as 15 minutes, depending upon conditions. I have found that the attention span of the average helmsman sailing upwind is about 45 minutes (allowing five minutes for settling in). Reaching creates the most strain on the helmsman; on a hard reach a helmsman may last 15 minutes before having to be rotated. Despite the powers of concentration required, a good downwind helmsman can go as long as 60 to 90 minutes.

Racers with dinghy experience tend to make good helmsmen because they do not oversteer and have a better understanding of how to deal with the waves. Nevertheless, under storm conditions it is better to rotate helmsmen often to keep interest alive. The skipper should be alert to signs of concentration deserting the helmsman (the boat wanders off course and slows down). With a good helmsman, the watch below will be able to relax and get needed rest. An inexperienced helmsman will often hit the waves with great force, causing turmoil below. In any case, the helmsman must avoid hitting waves head on and take a zigzag course of approximately 45 degrees to their breaking tops when going to windward. Continuous pounding causes breakdowns of both rig and crew.

If a boat's rudder is broken or otherwise out of action, you can still steer—using weight, balance, and sail trim. Moving the weight aft will reduce weather helm. Continuous adjustment of main and jib will help keep the boat on course.

The most difficult course to steer without a rudder is straight downwind, because there is a high chance of repeated jibes. The best way to sail downwind without a rudder is to wing the jib out to windward on a spinnaker pole. To help balance the boat downwind, make a drogue out of a small anchor, a canvas bucket, or a fender. Rig the drogue to the stern with a bridle by leading the lines to the two stern cleats. By taking up on either of the stern lines, the drogue can be moved from one side to the other to help steer the boat.

An emergency rudder can be rigged with the use of a boat hook or a spinnaker pole, and any solid, flat object, such as a chart table top, bunk board, or a dinette table (see the jury-rig section, page 125). Lash or bolt the board to the pole. You may need some sort of ballast to keep the rudder end in the water; a small anchor would do fine. Tie the whole assembly to the stern pulpit or bulwark and you may be able to steer well enough to keep a reasonable course to safety.

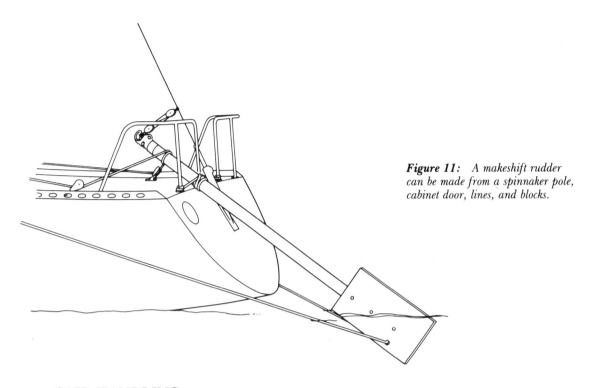

SAIL HANDLING
UNDER
STORM CONDITIONS

Traditionally, from the days of the square-rigged sailing ships to now, sail handling under storm conditions has been the most difficult and dangerous job a crew member can perform. The boat is a bucking, violent platform. The wind makes a fiendish thing out of a sail that seems to want to flog itself and the crew to pieces. Rain and seas sweeping over the boat do not make the sail change any easier. But at sea, it was ever thus—men climbed into the yards in the face of a rising gale to furl square sails, just as they go to the bow today on a racing or cruising boat to take down a jib that is overpowering the vessel.

Modern technology has made the job somewhat easier. Furling main and jib systems on cruising boats allow

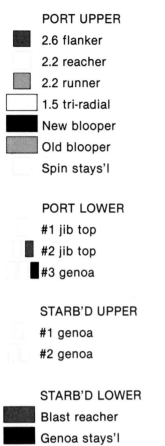

PORT UPPER

2.6 flanker

2.2 reacher

2.2 runner

1.5 tri-radial

New blooper

Old blooper

Spin stays'l

PORT LOWER

#1 jib top

#2 jib top

#3 genoa

STARB'D UPPER

#1 genoa

#2 genoa

STARB'D LOWER

Blast reacher

Genoa stays'l

Tall boy

#4 jib top

#5 jib top

Tack

Clew

Head

Figure 12: *Typical sail inventory as posted near the sail bins defines sails, sailbags, and parts of the sail by colors and shapes.*

shorthanded crews to deal with too much sail more quickly and more efficiently. The weight of canvas has been replaced by lighter Dacron, although anyone who has had to take down a large, wet, flapping genoa that threatens to go over the side may dispute that statement. Racing boats have larger crews to handle non-self-furling sails. Many cruising skippers still hank on their sails, because of a lack of faith in a furling system's ability to work perfectly in a storm emergency.

Storms, however, rarely come without warning. There is much that the wise skipper can do to prepare his boat and his crew well in advance of the crisis point. After heavy weather comes it is almost too late to perform tasks in an orderly fashion unless sails, gear, and crew are ready.

Preparation begins at the dock. Sails should be stowed ahead of time in a coded fashion, either in bins or in bags on hooks, but not piled helter-skelter in the forepeak where the sail that is needed may be on the very bottom of a heavy pile of sailbags. Color coding is a

Sail Chart

Mainsail
Drifter   (0-3)
Light #1 (3-13)
Heavy #1 (14-20)
          #2 (20-25)
          #3 (25-30)
          #4 (30+)
Reacher
    .5 oz. spinnaker
    .75 oz. spinnaker
    1.5 oz. spinnaker
Staysail
    .75 blooper
Storm trysail
Storm jib

prerequisite where there is a large sail inventory. Make sure to post the color coding where it is easily read. Sailbags should be labelled despite the coding. Some skippers even go as far as marking the sail at the tack or the clew.

Carefully review the sail inventory before leaving the dock so there is a sail on board for every condition. Make sure each sail is readily accessible and that every member of the crew knows not only where they are but the boat's procedures for sail change. Before leaving the dock, flake and roll the storm jib and trysail tightly into sausages and secure them with rubber bands. They'll be used in the worst of conditions, and this method keeps them under control as they are being raised and is also a good way to store them and get to them quickly.

Just before departure is also a good time to review harnessing and certain other safety procedures. It is mandatory on most boats that harnesses be worn on deck in advance of a rising storm, and that when a sail change has to be made, every available crew member be used and each be harnessed up. No cruising or racing boat should go offshore for an extended race or passage without making sure that a jackstay has been rigged inboard in some fashion for harnesses to be hooked to. And despite the storm conditions—the noise of the wind and the waves—some form of communication between crew members, even if only hand signals, must be established. Every movement by the crew should be deliberate and thoroughly understood by other crew members.

Underway, prepare storm sails for hoisting as soon as indications of approaching heavy weather are received. Reduce sail in advance, especially when you are cruising and time is not of the essence.

Careful planning of sail changes in advance on racing boats will pay off too. On *Boomerang*, during the 1982 Bermuda Race, we carefully watched what appeared to be a violent squall approaching, trying to determine whether its black clouds hid more wind than rain, or vice versa. We had sailed through several heavy rain-showers that morning but none contained strong winds. Up were a blast reacher, a small staysail, and a full main. The first step was to take one reef in the main as the storm approached.

For a few minutes, I pondered whether to drop the staysail, and as I delayed giving the order we were hit by lightning in advance of the squall. The top of the mast glowed as static electricity fired down the backstay over my head while I steered the boat. Then an electrical charge hissed across the sails followed by a tremendous clap of thunder. I was too stunned to react, the staysail remained up, and I had to bear off 90 degrees from our course with the wind blowing 48 knots apparent over the stern (about 60 true). The error on my part pushed us more than two miles below our rhumb line. I was more cautious in the next series of squalls.

The traditional way to change a headsail is to bring the boat into the wind and drop the sail to the deck as quickly as possible. Usually the sail is wildly luffing, however, which can result in damage to the sail or the crew. A better method of reducing force on the sails while dropping or changing them is to turn straight downwind. The sail is trimmed flat, and then is dropped. The main can also be dropped or reefed downwind if it is sheeted in to keep the battens off the shrouds. Commands can easily be heard, the boat is not plunging bow-on into breaking seas, and the entire sail change is accomplished in a much safer manner.

On the well-run boat, the skipper is always one or two sail changes ahead, the sails ready belowdecks to counter either heavier or lighter air. The boat itself should be ready, decks clear, with lines coiled or flaked.

In the 1977 Sydney-Hobart Race, *Kialoa* and *Windward Passage* were running neck and neck in clear air and light winds. A freak dry-air squall hit both boats, creating havoc on *Windward Passage*, which was unprepared. Soda cans on deck, lines, and sweaters and foul weather gear draped over the winches slowed her sail change. *Kialoa* was able to make the change in a few minutes, while *Passage* was forced to sail 180 degrees away from her course as the crew scrambled to sort out the mess.

When the weather is really rough, approaching gale conditions, get the bigger sail off and belowdecks before the replacement sail is brought up. On masthead rig yachts, the biggest sail is usually the genoa. On ketches, yawls, schooners, and modern fractional rig boats the mainsail is the larger sail.

If you are forced to drop the main, remember that the sail gives the mast considerable support. While the mainsail is coming down, slack the sheet two or three feet to luff the headsail and keep the pressure off the spar. If the boat is under headsail alone, use extra halyards as running backstays to help support the mast.

The use of grooved double headstays has become common, especially on racing yachts, so that one headsail can be dropped while the other is raised. It makes for an efficient, speedy sail change in normal weather; boat speed is kept up because there is always a headsail in place. But in gale force winds, the luff of a headsail can rip out of the groove in a headfoil. There should be an alternate method for keeping a storm jib on the headstay, such as the use of lanyards to keep it in place so that not all of the pressure is on the luff groove.

Setting a storm trysail can take a great deal of time under heavy weather conditions. Because it is usually done with the weather at its worst, the more crew available the faster it will go. Once the mainsail is lowered, secure the topping lift tightly, take the slack out of the mainsheet, and tie a line from the boom's outboard end to the leeward side of the deck, so there is no play in the boom at all. (The boom will help catch anyone thrown unexpectedly across the deck if it is in this position, Rod Stephens suggests.) Take the mainsail off the boom completely and stow it below.

Before the trysail is ready to hoist, be sure that it is clear; having it already furled, sausage-like, will speed

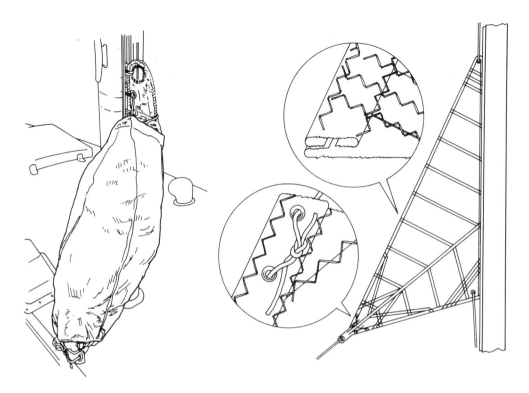

Figure 13: A storm trysail is ready in its bag attached to its own track on the mast (left). Strong construction in clew and stitching are among its features.

up the process. Feed the slides of the trysail on the mast track (some prudent skippers have a separate storm trysail track). Then secure the halyard and add the tack pennant and the sheets. The sheet is generally led through a block on the rail.

Some cruising boats keep the storm trysail permanently bent on. The trysail is stowed in a small bag with rain holes at the foot of the mast. When it is needed it is simply hoisted up and pulled from the bag, and its sheets attached and trimmed.

The tendency to carry sails too long is dangerous and foolhardy, even though it is a common fault among racing skippers. Robert Symonette, a longtime ocean racer and a member of the crew of *Tenacious* during the 1979 Fastnet, comments on that race: "On reflection, I do not think we should have waited so long to set a storm trysail and go to a smaller jib. The fact that we did not trust the smaller jib indicates a state of unpreparedness that a top-notch ocean racer should not have had to endure. We were saved by a number of excess safety factors and a tremendously competent and experienced crew."

Reefing

Most yachts now have a jiffy reef system that allows the mainsail to be reefed quickly at the gooseneck. Because each boat's reefing system is different, skippers must make sure that crew members know exactly how it works and what procedures are used.

In general, however, the biggest problems occur at the gooseneck, where the sail slides or luff rope are brought down to attach the new tack to the reefing hook. More problems occur at the outboard end of the boom while securing the clew.

Reefing quickly takes good coordination between the halyard handler and the crew member at the gooseneck; it should be done as speedily as possible to avoid damaging the cloth or breaking a batten. Secure leeward running backstays forward. Mark the halyard so that the crew knows exactly how much to lower it for attaching the tack and pulling the clew tight. When the reefing line on the clew is taken up, make sure no part of the sail itself is trapped between the clew and the boom. Always try to reef with as little air in the sail as possible. If the boat is going to windward, let out the main sheet so that the sail luffs, make sure the topping lift is eased, and go about it. The jib will keep the boat speed up.

Once the reefing lines are tight, secure the clew grommet to the end of the boom with another line or a sail tie. (Note that pad eyes and turning blocks on the boom that hold the reefing lines have been known to self-destruct under pressure.)

Check your reefing system at the mooring, or in light air. Make sure that the spaces between slides allow the reefing grommets to be brought to the reef hook on the

Every crew member on watch has an assignment aboard this racing yacht participating in the 1980 Sardinia Cup. The wind was clocked at 50 knots.
Daniel Forster

gooseneck tightly and securely, with no large gap in the luff above the hook when the halyard is taken up. Neither should there be excess material.

Stowing Sails

After a sail change, flake them and stow them below in their appropriate bags or bins. Larger sails may have to be flaked on deck and then quickly brought below.

It is not advisable to keep a foresail stowed on deck during a storm. On our way to Bermuda aboard the Merchant Marine Academy entry *Captive* in 1974, the crew had flaked down a headsail along the leeward rail. As water swept the deck and built up against the sail, the rail carried over the side—taking several stanchions and half the pulpit with it.

If you must keep a sail on the foredeck be sure it is lashed down on the windward side as far aft as possible. The sail should be flaked tightly using sail stops or lines with slip knots that can be taken out quickly. The line securing the sail to the boat should not be the same line used to furl it.

STORM TACTICS

When a storm is known to be approaching, especially when all signs point to a sustained storm of Force 10 conditions (50 knots plus) or worse, it's time to plan the next 48 hours and prepare for any eventuality.

During this period of relative calm while you're carrying enough sail to stay on course and keep moving, these preliminary preparations should be made:

1. Establish your position, either through celestial navigation or electronic navigation, or both.

2. Stow all unused sails and gear below.

3. Cook a simple, hot meal; put hot soup in thermos jugs; and drink no alcoholic beverages.

4. Make sure everything above and below decks is secure.

Once the storm hits there are four courses of action that can be taken to ride it out: Lying to a sea anchor, lying ahull, heaving to, and running with the storm. Among deepwater sailors who have experienced major storms there are partisans for each of these techniques, although the consensus seems to be that when all else fails and the boat is in danger from breaking seas, running off under bare poles is the best technique.

Lying to a Sea Anchor

A sea anchor is generally a large canvas drogue that will hold the boat's bow into the wind, thereby exposing the strongest and most streamlined part of the hull to the seas. A small riding sail on the mizzen mast or a storm jib hanked to the mainmast backstay will also help keep the boat's head into the wind.

One disadvantage to the drogue technique is that the vessel, because of pressure against the keel and windage aloft, may lie at right angles to the drogue—thereby exposing itself to beam seas and severe chafing of the drogue line.

Other disadvantages: a short-keeled yacht needs a riding sail to keep its head into the wind, but in extremely heavy conditions the sail may flog itself to pieces. And a rudder, when a boat is lying to a sea anchor, is under great strain as the boat makes sternway in heavy seas. Because the drogue line is extremely subject to chafing, a sail can be moused around the line and used as chafing gear.

Lying Ahull

This technique is a viable alternative for giving the crew a rest for a short period of time, in conditions less than Force 9 (44–47 knots). When lying ahull the boat skids slowly before the seas and wind without sails up. The tiller is lashed a little to leeward to keep the vessel's head from falling off. The boat will lie at right angles to the wind and the seas will be broad to the beam.

The main disadvantage to lying ahull is that once the beam seas begin breaking over the boat (Force 10 plus), the vessel is in jeopardy. Breaking seas can carry away pulpits, dinghies, and deck gear, and smash portlights or stave in a coachroof. Figure that every cubic meter of water contains slightly more than one ton of mass. A breaking wave may thus contain 500 tons or more, curling and racing downslope at speeds up to 20 to 30 knots. This downsloping, tumbling action of the sea creates the great danger of the boat rolling 360 degrees, with subsequent dismasting and frightful damage to the boat and possible injury to the crew. Another disadvantage to lying ahull is that to do it, the crew must button up the boat and stay below. The boat is subject to the whim of the waves and the crew is both psychologically and physically uncomfortable as the boat is buffeted in the wave troughs.

Heaving To

A much more comfortable method for riding out a storm is to heave to. The wind is brought on the weather bow and the vessel holds itself in that position, where she will ride most safely and easily unless the storm gets worse and the frenzy of the seas makes even heaving to untenable.

To heave to, bring the boat about without releasing the leeward jib sheet. With the headsail backed, lash the helm to leeward. The backed jib and opposing rudder will cause the boat to jog slightly to windward, then fall off, then come up again, making little headway and a lot of leeway. The motion will be easier and will afford the crew some rest as well as a feeling that the boat is dealing with the storm instead of being at its mercy. Typically, the boat will maintain an attitude of about 45 to 50 degrees off the wind and proceed forward through the water at an average speed of about a knot.

Heaving to has the advantage of keeping the boat's speed under control and reducing the impact of breaking seas.

Running with and Without Warps

If the storm increases and the boat's motion and behavior become erratic—and it's no longer safe to take a chance with breaking seas—the only option is to run with the storm under bare poles or with a small storm jib, to make the steering easier. Boat speed must be kept well under potential hull speed, to keep control, and this can be done by streaming warps—long, heavy lines of various sorts. The warps will also help to stabilize the boat directionally and prevent broaching and dangerous surfing in the short, very steep seas of the early phases of a severe storm. (Be careful the warps don't get caught in the rudder.) Boats with fin keels are particularly subject to broaching. Surfing down steep seas can result in a pitchpole—the extremely dangerous end-for-end tumble of a yacht.

There are a number of methods of using warps. Some cruising yachts carry tires on board for that purpose. Robin Knox-Johnson, winner of the 1968 Single-handed Non-stop Round-the-World Race, used a U-shaped bight of 100 fathoms of two-inch polypropylene rope when running before several storms.

In the 1979 Fastnet Race, several skippers reported that they were helped by trailing warps astern to slow their progress. But there was another school of thought that included *Williwaw*'s Dennis Conner and *Police Car*'s Chris Bouzaid, who both found it was far better to scoot along fast and keep good steerageway. "If you wallowed you were at the mercy of the waves," said Conner.

Heavy wind and high seas find the crew of this cruising boat protected by a dodger as the boat moves along under storm jib and double-reefed main.
Alastair Black

The disadvantage of running off is that the boat is presented stern to the seas, offering the vulnerable companionway hatch and cockpit to breaking waves aft. If your boat has a big cockpit with no reinforcing, no bridge deck, or no high lip at the companionway entrance, running off may not be for you. Considerable danger can result from a pooping wave filling the cockpit or smashing the washboards at the entrance to the companionway hatch.

Special Sail Rigs and Combinations

When carrying sail is still tenable, certain combinations may help keep the boat balanced and moving. Here are some thoughts:

A yacht increases weather helm as it heels, requiring reduction in the mainsail area for a given headsail as the wind increases. With a yawl or ketch, drop the mizzen, or leave the mizzen up and drop the main. This "split rig" is very effective in 25-plus winds. Even more effective is "centering" the sail area by the use of a staysail and reefed main.

When running, the disadvantages to twin headsails include considerable rolling, the necessity for two sets of twins for winds above and below 12 knots, the requirement that the wind be almost dead astern, the necessity for two poles and two halyards, and the time that it takes to set two poles.

When heaving to, a storm trysail on the mainmast will save deep-reefing the main and possibly save the sail itself. An alternate method is to hoist the storm trysail on the mizzen mast or hank it to the mizzen backstay to get the sail area aft, so that the bow will vane to windward. The trysail is sheeted forward. The disadvantage is that as the wind comes up the sail will begin to flog.

A double head rig does keep the sail area low. A boomless trysail and forestaysail combination makes jibing easier in heavy weather. The main boom must be tightly secured.

BEFORE DEPARTURE

When you are equipping and preparing a boat for heavy weather, whether at sea or before you leave, advance planning and forethought are essential. Be prepared so you can take what comes, even though you hope to be lucky and avoid extreme storms. Here are some lists that may be useful in getting your boat ready for heavy weather:

Pre-Sail Checklists

Safety Equipment

• *Harnesses* Have they been checked recently for metal fatigue or for worn or torn fabric?

• *PFDs* Do they meet Coast Guard standards? Is there one for every member of the crew, as required? Do you have enough of the kind with collars that support the head?

• *Life rafts* When was the last time they were checked for self-inflating? Do they contain survival equipment? What kind? Fresh water and provisions? (See Appendix A.)

CHAPTER 3

Living in Heavy Weather

• *Flares and other distress signals*   Is there a flare gun and flares on board? Other signaling devices? Mirrors? When was the flare gun last fired?

• *Buoys*   Is there a horseshoe buoy mounted on the rail so it can be tossed quickly to a person in the water? A Danbuoy (temporary emergency buoy) for marking the person's position? Strobe?

• *Communications*   Is the VHF in good working condition? Does everyone know the distress frequency on SSB and how to work the set? Is there an EPIRB (Emergency Position Indicating Rescue Buoy) on board? Is there one in the life raft?

• *Navigation equipment*   Is it all in good working order? Do you have the equipment you need?

• *Lifelines*   Check them for weakness. The stanchions should be through-bolted and bedded.

Rudder and Emergency

• *Steering*   Is the emergency tiller stowed where it can be put into service quickly? Is the crew trained to rig it?

• *Bilge pumps*   They should be large volume, one for the cockpit and one for below. Handles must be stowed where they can be grabbed quickly.

Rigging and Gear

• *Cockpit pad eyes*   Install them for use with safety harnesses.

• *Storm covers*   Lexan or wood to put over each port and cabin window.

• *Leaks*   Repair them on deck and around the mast base.

• *Hatches*   Are they watertight? Repair the ones that are not.

• *Dorade vents*   Are they operative?

• *Handholds*   Enough above and below?

- *Standing rigging* Check all fittings—tangs, turnbuckles, wire and rod rigging—for corrosion and fatigue.
- *Running rigging* Replace worn halyards and sheets. Check splices and blocks.
- *Sails* Check them carefully. Loose stitching and small tears can reduce a sail to shreds in heavy winds.
- *Shackles* Check for corrosion and wear. Keep spares on board.
- *Sheaves* Check the fittings; wear may cause a wire to jump the sheave.
- *Mast* Inspect all weldments and fittings.
- *Lights* Check all running lights and navigation equipment lights.
- *Seacocks* Check for seepage from worn gaskets, or valve corrosion. Each seacock should have a hull plug attached to it. Extra plugs in various sizes should be at hand.
- *Safety line* Rig one fore and aft on the centerline.
- *Flag halyard* Tape it to the mast or remove it.
- *Scupper drains* Do they drain quickly? Otherwise, flush them out.
- *Stuffing box* Be sure the proper equipment to tighten it is aboard.
- *Winches* Winches should be taken apart periodically and cleaned with fresh water to remove accumulated salt. If there is a problem with a winch often it is a broken part; carry extras. See page 131 for information about regular maintenance.

AT SEA

As soon as the prudent skipper becomes aware of an impending storm the crew should be assigned various jobs to get the boat ready for the onslaught—stowing and bringing out gear, preparing a hot meal and getting one-pot meals ready in advance. Start the engine and fully charge the batteries (make sure, by the way, that they are securely tied down; a rogue battery can destroy a boat's interior).

Next, the skipper should outline his course of action to the crew and discuss all procedures that may have to be carried out during heavy weather—watch system, sequence for shortening sail, provisions for rigging sea anchors, warps, etc. Review the boat's position and distance to go to its destination, plus alternate possibilities. The more the crew knows the better it will function; crew morale is the key to smooth operation during a storm. So is experience. The majority (preferably all) of the crew members must have the capacity to do whatever is required of them even if afflicted by *mal de mer*.

Belowdecks, the need for ample handholds and rails should be quite apparent. Any large space belowdecks should be broken up, either with heavy-weather lines or by some kind of midship railing.

Never overlook the fact that good rough weather ventilation below—as well as maintaining a clean engine and bilge—can help minimize seasickness (see page 82). Smoking should be prohibited belowdecks when living under battened-down conditions.

"It is challenging to test the limit of your boat, your equipment, your sails and yourself."

Screw-in deck plates should be available for all ventilators and fuel vents. The decision about how much in advance of the storm to install them, or whether to install them at all, is up to the skipper. The engine ventilators, in any case, should be covered—because if there is a knockdown the engine may be flooded.

Next, make sure that water will not come below. Secure the hatches and portlights. If you have storm shutters, check them, match them up, and install them. Fill the slots on the sides and bottom of the companionway hatch with quick-setting seam compound and jam the washboards into place at least to deck level. (Some owners drill a hole through the wooden border and the washboard and insert a bolt or large cotter pin to keep the board in place.) The object is to keep the boards

from falling out if a knockdown is sustained. Washboards should be heavy and should fit together with overlapping seams.

Have a crew member check the main bilge pump and pump the bilge dry. Get out the emergency bilge pump and assemble it, ready for use.

Put flashlights, odd pieces of line (short stuff), hand tools, nuts, bolts, screws, cotter pins, shackles, tape, rigging knife, and whistle in a ditty bag. Store it on deck where it is secure but quickly accessible.

Again below, the trick is to try to maintain dry bunks, dry changes of clothes, and protection for vulnerable food stores. Be sure you have one-pot hot meals available as discussed later in this chapter.

Belowdecks Checklist

The following suggestions may be helpful in making life belowdecks more tolerable during heavy weather.

• *Bunk boards or lee cloths* Be sure they fit. Have crew install them.

• *Lockers* Keep clothes dry by covering them with large plastic garbage bags. Close and secure lockers, ice box.

• *Sinks* Do they drain when the boat is heeled? If not, close the seacock and tell crew that you've done so and not to use the sink in question.

• *Stowage* Keep a record or a diagram of where everything is stowed.

• *Tools* Keep a saw, punch, and hammer, several sets of pliers, and screwdrivers in moisture-proof stowage and easily accessible.

• *Towels and facecloths* Number them for the crew.

• *Clothes* One dry change for about every 125 miles. Wrap deck shoes and socks in plastic bags.

• *Blankets and sleeping bags* Try to keep them dry. Stuff them in garbage bags if need be.

- *Bunks*   Make up bunks for the offwatch. Do not sit on the bunks with wet clothes and foul weather gear. Post a bunk list of who sleeps where.
- *Foul weather gear storage*   Wipe them off with a towel kept near the companionway hatch when coming below. Have a wet locker near the companionway.
- *General cleanliness*   Wash daily and keep up with your usual cleanliness routine. Pick up boat gear. Stow your personal gear; do not let it clutter the cabin.

FOOD

When a gale warning has been received, the cook should serve a good hot meal and also prepare a spare one-pot meal such as stew in addition to soup and sandwiches. Serve the stew 12 to 14 hours after the first hot meal. That, plus snacks of raisins, nuts, or chocolate and a still later meal of the soup and sandwiches, should get the crew through the first 24 hours. And if the pot holds two rations of stew the crew is set for 36 hours. By then, most storms will moderate enough to cook again. Have the crew help themselves. If necessary, secure the pot to the top of the stove with wire; keep its lid tight. Fried food should be avoided, because the smell of frying and the heaviness of the food itself tend to cause seasickness.

Hot water is a very important item. Fill several thermoses with hot water. It can be used by the crew to make tea, hot cocoa, or premixed soup. Consider staying away from coffee. It has no food value and tends to make some people seasick. Tea laced with honey, or hot water with honey, provides energy and often stays down when nothing else will.

Here are some notes about food and food preparation:

Precook food ashore, then freeze it, and stow in your boat's freezer if it has one.

Use deep pots with tops. Wire the pots to the stove.

Plan a heavy-weather meal and evening meals before you leave.

Cream of Wheat or any nutritional hot cereal is filling, warming, and nourishing. So is hot water plus chocolate mix and dry milk.

Icebox or refrigerator—pack it in layers to leave as little air around items as possible. Only the cook should rummage through it.

Food stowage—The cook and one member of the crew should do the job and then make a chart of the food disposition.

A pressure cooker is useful for making one-pot meals. Use it for preparing potatoes and vegetables.

Meals should be scheduled at regular times.

Clean up after every meal. Rotate the cleanup chores.

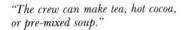

"The crew can make tea, hot cocoa, or pre-mixed soup."

CLOTHING

There are four requirements for proper seagoing clothing. The first of these is *comfort,* to allow the sailor to concentrate on tactics if he or she is racing, or getting from point A to point B in the best way possible if cruising. Comfort means not being overheated or chilled while going about tasks on deck or below.

The second requirement is *maneuverability.* The sailor needs freedom of movement, unrestricted by excessive layers, bulky wetsuits (dinghy racing) or heavy foul weather gear.

Minimum weight is the third requirement. Look for clothes with good insulation that are not heavy or cumbersome.

Safety is the fourth requirement. Wet suits help guard the dinghy sailor against hypothermia. Personal flotation devices such as float coats provide a measure of safety against it in case of capsize or being knocked overboard.

All crew members should have foul weather gear suitable for all conditions. As soon as a storm warning exists, crew members should break out the gear they will wear plus extra dry clothing, and stow it in plastic bags in readily accessible locations.

Foul weather gear should fit comfortably, and should ultimately keep you as dry as possible. There are a number of foul weather gear choices on the market, but in general the clothing should have these features: a waterproof outside layer, an inside layer that breathes, some sort of ventilation (probably in the armpit area), a high zipper covered by a flap, a collar high enough to cover the lower face when it is zipped, a complete hood with tightening strings, and sleeves with inside wrist cuffs. Bib overalls in the same fabric are best, because they keep the upper body dry; and pockets in the overalls are useful for carrying tools or a rigging knife. The best foul weather gear has welded or taped seams so that water cannot enter by capillary action. Foul weather gear

In big seas and gale-force winds, the sailor should not be on deck unless completely dressed in foul-weather gear and harnessed to safety lines.
John Mecray

that "breathes" is not waterproof and will not keep a crew member dry during hours of storm sailing.

All personal gear should be color-coded or numbered against a preset system, so crew can pick out their own clothing in chaotic conditions or at night. A strip of colored tape will do the job on foul weather gear.

Deck shoes and boots should have functioning non-skid soles. For offshore sailing, calf-high fisherman's boots worn without shoes are best because they can be kicked off quickly. A grommet in the backs of the boots is handy for hanging them up.

Float coats are warm and offer some flotation. Sew a small strobe light into the pocket of your float coat.

On your head, wear a fisherman's sou'wester in heavy, wet weather and a woolen watch cap when it is cold and dry. An oiled raw wool sweater resists water. However, wear a T-shirt under it to absorb perspiration.

Seagoing clothes should be quick-drying. Dacron dries faster than cotton, but cotton and wool are warmer and absorb perspiration. Polypropylene underwear, lightweight and considered effective in absorbing perspiration, is becoming popular. Dress in layers. A good, warm combination is thermal underwear and socks under wool pants and shirts, topped by a pile vest or jacket. The top layer should act as a windbreaker—it's usually a foul weather jacket.

STOWAGE

On the approach of bad weather, everything below should be secured. Examine the main saloon and sleeping quarters with a critical eye and imagine life at a sharp angle of heel, the boat pitching and tossing like a corkscrew. All gear, books, utensils, and personal items must be properly stowed, and lashed or wedged in place, heavy things generally down low. Galley storage cabinets must be closed tight, cupboard sliders shut, stove gimballed. Locker doors and drawers should be secured. Where there is only one water tank, a reserve of water should be carried in separate containers.

Do not use cardboard boxes for storage. They disintegrate and the wet pieces of cardboard wind up in the bilge where they can clog the bilge pump.

Pull all labels off cans and mark them with a permanent marking pen. Labels come off when the cans get wet and they too clog the bilge and, eventually, the bilge pump.

On deck, double-lash everything, particularly the life raft. Stow extra gear, cushions, extra lines, and hardware in appropriate lockers above and below decks.

SEASICKNESS

Motion sickness is caused by a conflict in the information provided to the brain by three systems of the body that deal with balance and position: the vestibular (labyrinth) system in the inner ear, the eyes, and certain position sensors in the joints and tendons. Most important are those sensors in the neck, which signal movement of the head.

In a rough sea, the vestibular system is stimulated in a chaotic fashion. A boat has six possible motions—three rotary (roll, pitch, and yaw) which primarily stimulate the semicircular canals of the inner ear, and three linear motions (surge, heave, and sway), which stimulate the body's position-sensing mechanisms. Combined rotary and linear motions cause seasickness. This combination of movements most often occurs when a boat is heading into a wave system.

When you receive information from the eyes and from the inner ear that departs from the usual pattern, or you are moved about in ways that the body hasn't learned to anticipate, you begin to feel ill.

Belowdecks, the eyes see only the movement within the cabin itself and not that of the whole boat. The boat's movement is reported to the brain by the inner ear. This results in a conflict of the senses and is accentuated by looking directly and precisely at something—reading, navigating, or cooking. Seasickness most often starts, or gets worse, when you go below.

On deck, the unfamiliar motion of the slow pitch, roll, and heave of the boat produces unfamiliar sensory information. Everyone with a normal inner ear can be made motion sick, but only a small percentage of the population is chronically susceptible to motion sickness and unable to adapt to a boat's motion after a few days. The cure, for most people, is time and the development of "sea legs"—the ability of the body to anticipate the boat's motion. Once you have sea legs, seasickness is usually cured.

Specialists say that how fast you get sea legs depends on sensitivity and adaptation. The brain eventually reconciles conflicting information, except for those who are never able to adapt. Reactions typically fall into four categories: the high sensitivity/fast adaptation (in which an individual has an initially severe reaction but will adapt rapidly), high sensitivity/slow adaptation (classic prolonged seasickness), low sensitivity/slow adaptation (period of prolonged early symptoms). Those with low sensitivity/fast adaptation are the fortunate ones.

It is a myth that seasickness can be controlled by diet. The stomach is an innocent bystander. There are three exceptions—drugs, food, or odors, which by themselves can cause nausea or lack of equilibrium. Alcohol is in this category and should be avoided. It may well be also that an empty stomach can increase the risk of seasickness. (This is not to say that the person should load up on food.)

It is also a myth that air and body temperature (including the feeling of being cold) are a cause of seasickness. Nor does the removal of ear wax have any effect one way or another on feeling ill. Emotional stress and anxiety may worsen the situation, but the basic cause of seasickness is not psychological.

Three factors determine whether a person gets seasick: size of the vessel, sea conditions, and individual susceptibility. Early symptoms of seasickness include: skin pallor, cold sweating, headache, malaise, dizziness, and vague abdominal discomfort. Recognition of these symptoms is important as this is the last chance to prevent further illness before the person becomes actively sick.

Other symptoms to watch for include: a very slow reflex response to the unfamiliar vision and motion stimulus, apathy and drowsiness first, then nausea, vomiting, and salivation. There is a serious problem if a crewman vomits repeatedly over a period of days because of the loss of fluid and electrolytes causing dehydration. Children are more susceptible to chronic vomiting because of their small body size. Thus the risk of dehydration is greater.

What should you do about seasickness? Know which of your crew are predisposed to it. Try to anticipate sickness-inducing situations, and react to the earliest symptoms of yawning, drowsiness, salivation, and stomach awareness by limiting sensory conflict and using anti-motion-sickness drugs.

Encourage the potentially sick crew to stay on deck, amidships, as the sensory conflict is inevitably greater below. Minimize time in the cabin. If the crew member must go below, tell him to look out a hatch or port to get a wide view. Restrict head movements, as this eliminates problems with the position sensors in the neck.

Have the potentially sick crew avoid reading and other visual tasks. Give them something active to do to keep their minds off of the abnormal motion. Taking the helm is good. The helmsman has both a distracting task and a need to look at the horizon or land, allowing the inner ear and the eyes to register the same motion, which has a stabilizing effect on the individual.

Try to give the sick crew something to eat, but avoid alcohol because it will alter vestibular function.

As a last resort, have the sick individual lie down below, face up, eyes closed, as close to the middle of the boat as possible. This may help but also slows down the adaptation process. Some people can hasten adaptation by sleeping aboard the boat the night before the voyage.

Medication should be rapidly effective without significant side effects such as drowsiness. (Keep non-oral as well as orally administered medication available.) Seasick drugs all act by diminishing sensitivity, thus giving the person a chance to adapt to abnormal motion before becoming sick.

Ideally, however, at the first gale warning, everyone should start anti-seasickness medication. It must be taken as a preventive measure, not as a cure. And each crew member should be responsible for bringing the medication that suits his or her needs best.

HYPOTHERMIA

Hypothermia is a factor in heavy weather sailing in two major instances—if a member of the crew goes overboard in cold water and suffers from exposure before being rescued, or if a crew member on watch is improperly dressed, becomes extremely chilled, and is unable to function. The first instance, obviously, is more serious than the second and normally would require medical help. But unless a member of the crew is a physician, there is usually no medical help on board. Skippers, therefore, should recognize the signs and know how to give aid to crew suffering from hypothermia.

Simply, hypothermia is a subnormal temperature within the central body. When the core temperature reaches 90 degrees Fahrenheit, heart failure can cause death. Drowning will occur if the person is in the water. In hypothermia, the body goes through an involuntary reaction to cold, one aspect of which is a decrease in blood circulation to the extremities in order to conserve heat in the body's core. Improper warming techniques such as massaging the limbs can bring on a further drop in the body's core temperatures and possibly heart stoppage. This occurs when cold, stagnant blood from the extremities returns to the core of the body, dropping the core temperature below the level that will sustain life.

Once it has been determined that a person is hypothermic (confused, disoriented, comatose), especially after immersion, move him belowdecks. Place the victim on a hard, flat surface (cabin sole will do) to allow the administration of CPR (cardiopulmonary resuscitation)

if needed. Handle the person gently and do not give anything to drink, especially alcohol. Gently remove all wet clothing. Apply heat to the central core of the body (head, neck, sides, and groin). Wrap warm, moist towels around these areas. Use warm water, not hot. Hot water bottles and blankets can also be used. Blankets will conserve but not add heat; an auxiliary source of heat is necessary.

One or two of the crew can take off their clothes and help to warm the naked victim with their own body heat by getting into a sleeping bag or wrapping up in a blanket with the victim.

The case may be less serious—a crew member has gotten chilled on watch and is showing preliminary signs of hypothermia such as confusion or disorientation. Get him below and into dry clothes and provide warm non-alcoholic drinks. Do not rub the victim's extremities or force exercise. One way of preventing these occurrences is to change watch sections more frequently when the weather is extremely cold and wet.

To prevent hypothermia wear a wet suit, especially in dinghies if the air or water temperature is below 60 degrees Fahrenheit. Wear a wool watch cap (it keeps the heat in) and a PFD.

If your boat has capsized or swamped but is floating, stay with it and try to climb out of the water as much as possible. The body loses heat 90 times faster in cold water than in still air of the same temperature. The PFD holds the person safely in one place so there is no need to swim or tread water, which cools a person 35 percent faster than when he stays still. The average person wearing light clothing and a PFD may survive as long as 2½ hours in 50 degree water by quietly remaining in the fetal position. The fetal position helps protect areas of high heat loss (sides, groin, neck, and head).

Huddling side by side in a circle, if there are several people in the water, will also help to conserve body heat. (See diagram, Appendix C.)

ON WATCH

When getting ready for a race or any long passage, the skipper must consider, along with his other chores, what system will be used for standing watches. His decision will be dictated by crew makeup and number and by the length of the passage or race. In general, however, two systems seem to be the most popular: "watch on watch" (four hours on and four hours off) and the Swedish system (which allows for five changes of watch in a 24-hour period).

Personally I favor four hours on and four hours off because the period off watch is long enough for getting rest, and the time on watch is short enough not to be overly fatiguing and cause the crew to lose concentration. Some skippers schedule six-hour watches during the daylight hours and four-hour periods during the night, but this system has the disadvantage of not routinizing the watch periods, so the body is not able to

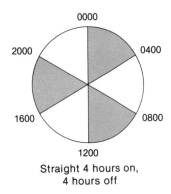

Straight 4 hours on,
4 hours off

Watches alternate times each day

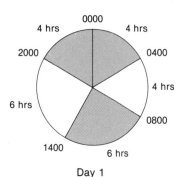

Day 1

4 on, 4 off at night
6 on, 6 off during day

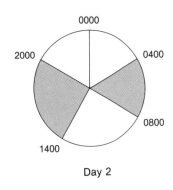

Day 2

| | Starboard watch | | Port watch |

Figure 14: *The diagrams show the three-day rotation of a four-on, four-off watch.*

deal physically with rest and wakefulness in the short bursts required.

Two versions of the Swedish system use a fairly good five-watch schedule, however. One breaks up the time periods into watches of 4, 6, 6, 4, and 4 hours, and the other into watches of 4, 4, 5, 6, and 5 hours. Typical watch bills would look like this: 1. 0200–0600, 0600–1200, 1200–1800, 1800–2200, 2200–0200; and 2. 0000–0400, 0400–0800, 0800–1300, 1300–1900, 1900–2400.

In these two schedules, the offwatch usually eats just before coming up on deck, the shortest watches are during the coldest, darkest hours, and the longest watches are during the day when the crew is accustomed to being awake anyway.

On a boat that is shorthanded, the watches can also be divided into three groups standing watch periods of six hours on and three hours off. This will work in short and medium distances but will tire out a crew on races or passages of more than 36 hours duration.

Notes on Watch Standing

Rotate positions amongst the crew during watch periods. This keeps interest and morale high and also helps the time pass more quickly. The rougher the weather, the more often the helmsman should be rotated. In the heaviest of conditions, as mentioned, 15 to 30 minutes is the maximum time a crew member should steer.

Friendly competition between the two watches—like which had the higher boat speed—also boosts morale and makes passages more interesting. It seems as if races are always lost on "the other watch." The "other watch" always steers an unsteady course, rips the sails, runs out of wind, has the wrong sail up.

The watch below is responsible for repairing ripped sails and broken gear, checking the bilges, and, in some systems, cooking the meal for the watch coming off. The watch below should be prepared to be called on deck for an emergency, but the watch on deck should refrain from an "all hands" call unless one is essential. The off watch should rest as much as it can; a watch that is called on deck too frequently will be ineffective when its turn comes to man the wheel and deal with sail trimming and sail changes. If the off watch *is* called, try to let the watch captain rest, as it is that person's responsibility to make the most decisions during his watch.

Plan to be on deck at least five minutes prior to your watch to get acclimated to conditions, and be filled in by the person you are relieving. Look carefully at the chart before coming on deck and decide upon your objective during your spell. It is important that the log book be kept up to date and that weather forecasts are listened to regularly. All watch members should have a function and be made to feel that they are part of the action.

Plan meals around watch changes. In the four-on four-off system, breakfast should be served to the ongoing watch at 0730; the offgoing watch takes its meal at 0800 and rests until lunch, which it eats at 1130. The next offcoming watch eats at 1200. Dinner often takes a little longer because the stories are best. Some of my most pleasurable memories of sailing have been at the dinette table after coming below from a long afternoon of sailing. Dinner is served at 1930 for the ongoing watch and at 2000 for the watch leaving the deck. During their midwatch at night, the offwatch should have coffee and hot soup available for the watch coming below, and to fortify themselves against the cold and the darkness on deck.

Crew Attitudes

Disciplined watches may be one of the keys to a well-run boat, but attitudes on the part of the crew are the keys to discipline. Because a crew will obviously not function well if its morale is low, one of the skipper's jobs is to keep morale up so the boat will complete its passage or survive a storm well.

In rough weather, everything is difficult—from cooking an egg to putting on foul weather gear. Making a sail change, tying a knot, walking from one part of the boat to another, even going below take great effort. Apathy and drowsiness from seasickness are often present. Other factors that contribute to a negative attitude are: the cold, wet bedding and clothes, the fact that everyone else also looks miserable, constant violent motion and the shrieking of the storm, and the inability, as one sailor noted, "to separate enough air from the water to survive."

Fear of the unknown often leads to breakdown. "Is this the ultimate storm?" the crew member or skipper asks, having had no previous experience with anything worse. The skipper questions himself: "Are my storm tactics right? Will the boat hold together?" The skipper must pace himself and be an example to the crew until the worst of the storm is over. Because it may be 12 to 48 hours before this happens, experience and self-confidence play a major role in keeping the boat going.

"One of the skipper's jobs is to keep morale up so the boat will survive a storm well."

Fatigue may lead to errors and low morale. Be particularly careful when tired. Double check everything and make sure that watch captains do the same. It's possible to go without sleep for long periods provided you have some time just to stretch out and rest.

Be in good physical condition so that when the storm hits you will have the stamina to keep going. Protect yourself from the sun, drink small amounts of water frequently, use alcohol sparingly if at all. Take care of your hands; wear gloves and use hand lotion. Salt water driven into cuts on the hands will make them useless and you can't afford that. Don't take chances with seasickness; as mentioned, if a storm is on the way and you feel you might be susceptible, take medication immediately.

Make sure the boat is organized and neat both above and below decks. Check that the crew has stowed sails, sheets, tools, and personal gear. Harnesses are mandatory on deck and everyone not needed outside should stay below to keep warm and dry until called. Keep warm, but not with bulky clothing that will restrict movement. In cold weather wear a wool sweater, watch cap, long underwear, wool socks, and lined rubber gloves as well as foul weather gear.

As skipper you must be helpful and supportive so that crew members will do the same. Don't carry out any operation without planning it ahead of time. Talk each operation through with everyone involved so it will take minimum time and effort. If you are feeling strong, help those who are suffering from the storm. Don't be afraid to ask for help if you are on deck and feeling too weak or chilled to carry out an action.

Finally, use storm conditions to build experience for tougher future storms. Think of progress made as a morale builder. If you have been besieged by gale-force winds for 12 hours, let everyone know that you are half-way through the ordeal. Don't lose your sense of humor. "Who wants to sail around the world?" Ted Turner once asked his crew in the midst of a bad storm. No one replied but there were a lot of chuckles as the boat crashed through the waves. Everyone knew that storms in the Southern Ocean would be far worse than the one they were in.

As bad as any storm might seem, keep in mind that storms always end. It is remarkable how quickly spirits rise on a bright morning. In no time, wet blankets and wet cushions appear on deck. Wet clothing hangs in the rigging as the crew takes the sun. The nightmare of the past hours or days soon becomes a memory—one more bit of knowledge to add to the experience of sailing.

ELECTRONIC NAVIGATION

The basic tools of navigation are familiar to any skipper who ventures offshore—compass, depth sounder, timepiece, sextant, plotting tools, sumlog—and he certainly should not go to sea without knowing how to use them. The traditional forms of navigation, coastal or celestial, are visual; and today they are supplemented by electronic aids that can pierce through fog, storms, and poor visibility and come up with a position.

More than half a century of electronic development has produced reliable navigation gear that is lightweight, inexpensive, and easy to use, affording the navigator more precise data on a constant basis. But electronic gear can fail and the skipper must be able to rely on the basic techniques and tools, even though he may have an array of equipment in his nav station that costs a third of the price of his boat.

CHAPTER 4

Navigation: Electronic and Otherwise

Navigation in heavy weather begins well before the barometer plummets—in fact it begins when the nav station is being laid out. The area should be designed for efficiency and comfort, and proper navigational tools should be there for intended routes of passage.

The ultimate navigation station could include radar, Loran C, satellite navigation, wind and speed instruments, weatherfax (see the Weather chapter), all-band receivers, and programmable calculators. All this gear could easily be installed in a 40-footer, and would provide the capability to handle any navigational situation. At the other end of the spectrum are the minimum aids no vessel should leave home without: adequate speed- and distance-measuring devices, RDF, depth sounder, and basic piloting tools.

Depth sounders and RDFs are the most basic of the essential electronic navigational instruments, and properly used they can provide information for safe coastal piloting.

Depth sounders are reliable and inexpensive, and have a wide range of uses. They are useful when closing on a shoreline, or transiting harbors and bays. Although a depth sounder doesn't predict obstructions ahead, there is comfort in watching its bottom contour readings in the nav station or on a display in the cockpit. A recording depth sounder goes even further by providing a permanent record of depths traversed, so you can annotate particular soundings or match depth against time, and factor this into your dead reckoning.

Once a depth sounder is corrected to zero depth it is usually maintenance free. Caution should be exercised in misreading multiple blips. The depth is measured by bouncing signals off the bottom. Inaccuracies occur in shallow waters when these signals make two or three round trips resulting in multiple readings. With a little practice and adjustment of the gain, these types of misleading signals can be recognized.

During heavy weather, good soundings can enable the navigator to follow a particular bottom contour and

"The nav station should be designed for efficiency and comfort. Proper navigational tools should be there for intended routes."

"The hand-bearing compass is one of the navigator's most useful tools."

stay in deeper water till the weather moderates. If your depth does not match up with what is charted you are now alerted to potential errors in dead reckoning. Either way, judiciously used a depth sounder is the major electronic device for keeping your vessel off the bottom.

Throughout the world, coastal radiobeacons give navigators another kind of vital position information. With a *radio direction finder*—RDF—navigators can obtain their lines of position in any weather at any time. With these RDF bearings, coupled with depth-sounder and dead-reckoning information, a vessel can be safely navigated in most coastal environs.

98 Storm Sailing

An RDF is basically a radio with the ability to sense the direction a signal is coming from. Used with a compass an accurate LOP is obtained. Like the sextant, however, the RDF is a peculiar instrument and needs a bit of understanding and practice to be used effectively. Stations are situated around the world in strategic spots, emitting signals anywhere from ten miles to 200 miles. During heavy-weather passages the navigator may use these either to close with the coast or to parallel it. Depending on the deviation characteristics of an RDF, it is usually more accurate to catch signals ahead and behind or close to the beam, particularly on sailboats, where masts and rigging may bend the signals being received.

During the Fastnet Race of 1979, many navigators opted for hand-held RDFs that are waterproof and can be carried on deck. Ahead and behind bearings were successfully taken on various stations on the Irish coast and English coast, enabling navigators to safely round Fastnet Rock and the Scilly Islands during the height of the storm. It is also worthy of note that under RORC racing rules, depth sounders and RDFs are the only electronic aids allowed for the Fastnet Race.

While using an RDF the navigator should be mindful of errors due to land effect or night effect. Simply speaking, the radio signals will bend somewhat when passing over land. It is best to measure a signal which is sent directly off the coast rather than one coming from an inland station, or one that passes over intervening land. Night effect refers to erroneous signals generated by the change in the ionosphere. When plotting the radio bearing, you should apply a correction if the station is over 50 miles away. The signal is generated as a great circle and will require a slight correction when being applied to a mercator projection.

When setting up the ultimate nav station, *radar* provides the ultimate for use in heavy weather piloting. Piloting in restricted visibility becomes more comforting with the capability of "seeing" the world around you. Good radar can provide pictures up to 24 miles in range.

Aside from keeping you abreast of potential traffic situations the radar is an indispensible tool in coastal navigation. By showing distance off and bearings on headlands, it allows the navigator to plot real-time situations accurately and make corresponding adjustments to dead reckoning. As with RDFs, radar is subject to inaccuracies and should be used accordingly.

The best of the electronic position-finding tools available to the navigator are satellite navigation (*satnav*) and *Loran C*. State-of-the-art gear is relatively inexpensive, small, lightweight, and maintenance free. Satnav operates off satellites and can provide accurate positions worldwide to less than two nautical miles. Most satnavs provide DR updates and, depending on satellite passes, position updates anywhere from 20 minutes to every three or four hours. In terms of heavy weather accuracy and ease of use, satnav frees the navigator to monitor weather changes and attend to guiding the vessel.

In the typical nav station of an offshore racer, or cruising boat, the navigator has both electronic and traditional tools at his fingertips. Gary Jobson

Loran C is highly accurate—generally to within at least 500 yards—and has the capability of continuous update in all weather and conditions. It is oriented in the northern hemisphere and within a 500-mile band off most coasts. It is useful as a position-finding tool, and most up-to-date sets also give passage tracking, set and drift information, and waypoint information.

NAVIGATION: Otherwise

Navigation, coastal or offshore, is relatively easy in fine weather. Offshore, electronic navigation aids such as Loran C and satnav give us our position and send us on our way to the next point in the ocean—an invisible intersection of latitude and longitude that has as much meaning as a familiar street-crossing at home. If the electronics fail in clear weather because of a power outage (and they often do), the navigator uses his eyes and a sextant to find the boat's position from celestial bodies. Along the coast, dead reckoning is used to keep a track and in clear weather the boat's position is fixed by a number of piloting techniques involving the use of aids to navigation (buoys, lighthouses, towers, landmarks on shore), with reference to charts of the area.

But when the weather deteriorates and electronic aids give questionable readings, or no readings at all, the navigator's work assumes even more than its usual importance. As fog enshrouds the boat, or a storm approaches, the navigator will have pinpointed the boat's position so that the vessel can either continue its passage through the fog without standing into danger, or take up its course when the storm abates.

It is not our purpose to teach coastal piloting or celestial navigation. Most readers of this book already have the navigational knowhow to go to sea or make a coastal passage with safety, and others will probably be obtaining it through study and experience. And piloting/ navigation courses or a standard reference book like

Chapman's *Piloting, Seamanship & Small Boat Handling* (Hearst Marine Books, New York) will give still further study. There are, however, certain points that skippers and navigators should keep in mind in advance of bad weather—well before the boat enters storm or low-visibility conditions.

TOOLS

Every boat must be equipped with the appropriate tools for navigation. The tools can be divided into those that are part of the boat's essential equipment and those that are in the navigator's own toolkit. On most boats the two groups overlap, although the navigator may have certain items which are his own personal favorites.

The following items should be mandatory on every boat that puts to sea:

• Compasses: While a dinghy often may not have a compass (and many do), every boat intended for cruising or racing generally carries a ship's compass mounted in a binnacle if the boat has wheel steering, or mounted in a bulkhead or other spot where the helmsman can see it clearly if the boat is steered with a tiller. The compass must be accurate and should be professionally adjusted (swung) at least once a year. The compass is not only used for keeping a course, but for computing wind angles, bearings, and the like. It should be lit with a red bulb for night use and the cardinal points and numbers should be large enough to be seen at a glance by a helmsman in bad weather.

Some boats are not so equipped, but every vessel should also carry a hand-bearing compass. A good one not only backstops the ship's compass but is used for taking bearings against collision, on navigation aids to provide a fix, or on points of danger that need to be skirted. The hand-bearing compass is one of the navigator's most useful tools.

• Depth contour: In bad weather, as discussed earlier, working with the depth sounder lines on a chart, the navigator can find a DR position and set a course to keep the boat out of danger. In good weather, a bearing taken on a navigation aid coupled with a charted depth reading can provide a line of position.

Modern electronic depth sounders rarely fail, but as they operate off the ship's battery, there should be on board an alternate means of finding depth. Before the electronic depth sounder, which essentially bounces a signal off the bottom and measures the time of its return which it converts into feet or fathoms, there was the leadline. The leadline, usually made of rope, is marked in feet and fathoms, either in the traditional way with cloth and leather strips, or with plastic tags denoting feet. The leadline is especially useful at slow speed, probing a fogbound anchorage. The leadline has a hollow weight at the end which can be filled with tallow or grease to give some indication of the holding ground.

• Logs: To estimate distance covered, distance to go, and a number of other piloting functions involving time, speed, and distance, the seagoing boat should have a log—a device that simply clicks off the nautical miles the boat has covered through the water. As an onboard instrument, the log receives its power and gives its speed/distance message by means of a tiny paddlewheel mounted in a watertight through-hull opening. While distance can be computed by measuring the difference between two fixes or navigation aids on a chart, a log will give you a reasonably accurate idea of how close you may be to that important harbor entrance buoy when you are running in bad weather.

A taffrail log is based on similar principles except that the propeller is streamed from a long flexible cable that transmits to a gauge mounted on the boat's transom. Its major fault is that it is subject to fouling.

"Before the depth sounder, there was the lead line."

A totally different kind of log (but with the same derivation) is the deck log—a record of the boat's hour-by-hour and day-to-day progress from the time it leaves port to the time it returns home. The deck log is a legal record and should show no erasures; any changes should be made by putting a line through the original material.

104   Storm Sailing

Each day's entries should be signed by the skipper, although on most boats the actual entries for each watch are made by the watch captain.

The deck log usually is set off in columns beginning with the distance log notation for the time of entry. Other entries include compass course, barometric pressure, sea state, weather conditions, temperature, and visibility. Entries should be made hourly and at each change of watch, but they are also made when passing or taking bearings on a navigation aid or landmark, sail changes, meeting another vessel, or any non-routine happening. On a voyage away from home, the deck log should have a notation for days spent in port; also, comments from the watch are always useful in reconstructing what transpired during a passage or a race. The same book may contain an engine log and a radio log, although most vessels going offshore maintain a separate radio log for VHF and SSB transmissions that will also show emergency or distress communications.

If the motion of the boat is too violent or everything is too wet, consider using a tape recorder to dictate the hourly log while the facts are still fresh in your mind. This allows you to keep a good running record of events that can be transcribed later into the permanent logbook. Using a tape recorder will ensure that no event is overlooked, and that the log is not messy and unreadable later. Be sure to carry plenty of tapes and extra batteries along, and stow recorder and its gear in a plastic bag.

• Tools of the trade: Every navigator has his or her own favorite devices, but in general these are parallel rules, triangles, or some other plotting device, ruling off courses and keeping a DR track. Other necessary tools include a pair of dividers, sharp pencils, an accurate watch or chronometer, a time/speed/distance calculator, and a pair of binoculars; there are also new electronic calculators programmed for diverse navigation and piloting situations. An offshore navigator will carry his own sextant, plotting sheets, and any other tools and almanacs that he will need for offshore work.

• Publications: No boat should go to sea for coastal or offshore passages without certain minimum publications. These include:

Charts for the area and for other nearby areas to which the boat may be driven because of storms. One boat heading for Bermuda from Ft. Lauderdale, Florida, was forced to head back to Florida because of gear failure onboard. Unfortunately, it did not have charts for Jacksonville, to which it was bound in extremely bad weather; it was therefore forced to call the Coast Guard for guidance into the harbor.

Tide Tables and *Tidal Current Charts:* These are especially important in latitudes with a wide tidal range and strong current flow, and are available from the National Oceanic and Atmosphere Administration in Washington, and from its licensed distributors across the country. Private publications like *Eldridge's* and *Reed's Nautical Almanac* contain tide and current information for New England and the Middle Atlantic states.

Light Lists: Published by the Coast Guard, the *List of Lights and Other Marine Aids* provides complete information and characteristics of every aid to navigation in U.S. waters maintained by the Coast Guard and privately. The *Lists* are very handy when a buoy turns up that is not shown on the chart, or when you are searching for a particular light and discovering that its characteristics do not correspond with those on the chart. *Light Lists* do not appear every year and should be kept updated with the Coast Guard's weekly *Notice to Mariners.*

Coast Pilots: There are eight covering the entire United States coastal waters, published by the Coast

Guard. *Coast Pilots* contain information for which there is no room on a chart—such as details on harbors, obstructions to navigation, channel depths, siting of facilities for mariners, and approaches to harbors from the sea and their difficulties. This last is all-important to a vessel outside of its own home area trying to outrun a storm to safety or wanting to make port during bad weather.

Hydrographic Agency: A branch of the Defense Mapping Agency in Washington, the Hydrographic Agency publishes, among other works, Pub. 9, *The American Practical Navigator,* a traditional and invaluable guide for navigators written by Nathaniel Bowditch in 1799 and updated and revised ever since. The Agency also publishes sight reduction tables used for celestial navigation.

The experienced navigator, however, uses more than these specific tools to bring the vessel in his charge from Point A to Point B. Because navigation is an art as well as a science he will also, for instance, observe the steering abilities of the helmsman on watch to see how closely he or she clings to the course and how much steering error should be computed for the watch. He will be aware of currents and their effect on the boat, and of wave action and its effect on the helm. He will be awake to the boat making leeway. Before the onset of a storm he will have fixed the boat's position, and during bad weather he is responsible for knowing, within reason, where the boat is at all times. He should predict landfalls and pass the word to the watch on deck.

During storm conditions the navigator consults with the skipper on whether to run for shelter or head for the open sea. (In general, where the tidal stream opposes the wind, especially where there are shoals or dangerous inlets, the prudent tactic is to stay well out to sea until conditions improve.) But through all this it remains the navigator's job to bring his boat home safely.

All yachtsmen when putting to sea to race or cruise, whether it be for a day or a week, or more, should pay attention to weather forecasts either via VHF (NOAA weather radio) or locally. Most racing skippers do this as a matter of routine so that they can plan tactics. In fact, major offshore races are usually preceded by weather briefings at skippers' meetings. The briefing officer may be a government or private meteorologist, and he will bring all the data at his disposal to forecast conditions during the race—including satellite photographs and infra-red prints showing current flow.

Cruising sailors may not have access to this information, but both cruising and racing sailors should know not only how to interpret forecasts, but how to interpret what they see in the sky and the sea and what they feel in the wind. Sailing is certainly easier if the crew knows in advance what to expect—changes of wind, oncoming heavy weather, the possibility of poor visibility and fog.

A boat need not have anything more on board than a barometer, wind speed indicator, wind direction indicator or mechanical wind vane, and a thermometer to aid the skipper in forecasting weather changes. Many

CHAPTER 5

Weather

offshore yachts also carry weatherfax equipment, which receives weather maps transmitted from 40 to 50 stations in 20 countries. The transmissions can be of several kinds of charts and must be received via a single sideband radio capable of receiving radio frequencies from 3 kHz to 30 kHz. The charts include surface weather analysis, which predicts highs and lows for a given region and indications of system speed and direction. A weather prognosis chart predicts future weather patterns for a 24- to 36-hour period. And an extended weather map will show storm-system positions for the following two to five days.

All the means of forecasting that the skipper has—weather signs, instruments, and maps—are useless, however, unless he or she understands how to interpret them. It is not the purpose of this chapter to deliver a treatise on meteorology (there are many excellent texts available for study) but to provide some understanding of what the weather tools can tell you.

THE BAROMETER

The barometer most commonly used on board is the aneroid type—a non-liquid device that contains one or more metal capsules. The capsules are almost devoid of air and their minute expansion when the atmospheric pressure falls is magnified and transmitted, through a linkage, to a pointer that ranges over a dial. The dial should be calibrated in millibars (mb) to be in harmony with weather-service practice worldwide. A barometer that has a cylindrical chart attached to it is called a barograph; the chart is useful in keeping a record of the barometer's rise and fall.

Commenting on the 1979 Fastnet Race, crewman Robert Symonette said "I think we made a great mistake on *Tenacious* in not keeping the barograph operative. While I'm sure that most of the experienced people on on board sensed that something was wrong or about to go wrong, I am also sure that a glance at the barograph every half hour would have made us more aware of what was happening."

Taken by themselves, individual readings of the barometer have very little meaning. What is really important is "tendency"—the change in readings over a three-hour period that will help confirm or deny that you are heading for trouble. The following are rules of thumb when recording and analyzing falling barometric tendencies. Keep in mind that a fall in barometric pressure in lower latitudes has a greater effect on the strength of the wind than in higher latitudes.

TABLE 2

Implications of a Fall In Barometric Pressure

Tendency	Inference
Fall approaching 1 mb/hr (0.03 in/hr)	Looks as if a depression is coming.
Fall approaching 2 mb/hr (0.06 in/hr)	Expect Force 6 any time.
Fall approaching 3 mb/hr (0.10 in/hr)	Expect Force 8 any time.
Fall more than 3 mb/hr	Put into practice what you have already learned about the survival of small boats at sea.

FRONTS AND DEPRESSIONS

The air circulating around and toward a low-pressure center will consist of batches of warm and cold air. The latter, being denser than the former, will tend to wedge under it and so force it upwards. This constitutes a cold front and is normally associated with the formation of clouds and precipitation. The location of these cold fronts can be determined by the meteorologist from such information as a swift change in wind direction,

Weather   **111**

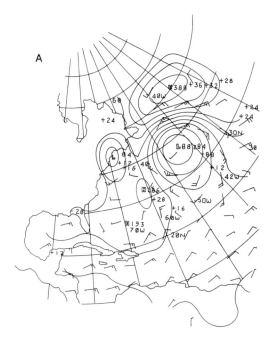

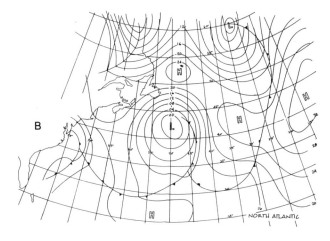

Figure 15: *Three typical weather charts received on weatherfax are North Atlantic Surface Analysis (A), frontal systems in the North Atlantic (B), and a wind speed and direction chart (C).*

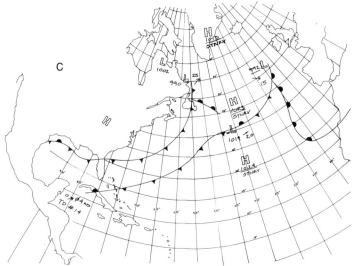

A weatherfax machine supplies visible up-to-date weather information. Alden Marine Fax III

or humidity and temperature changes. Warm fronts can be formed in a similar manner, as can occluded fronts, which result from the combining of a cold and warm front.

To the sailor, the approach of fronts means weather changes that may be severe. Weather signs and weather charts tell of their approach. In forecasting weather changes, the main signs to study are clouds and wind. Usually, the clouds will point to wind shifts if you study them carefully.

CLOUDS

Cirrus clouds (high, white delicate filaments) are among the best natural long-range weather forecasters. They appear ahead of approaching fronts and their attendant depressions. And they usually appear far enough ahead so that slow craft such as small boats can seek shelter.

Contrails are formed when aircraft fly in the deck of the atmosphere that we normally associate with cirrus clouds. Contrails show you the state of the upper atmosphere. Be suspicious if the contrails are slow to disappear. Watch for cirrus to form, showing an approaching front.

You can also tell the wind direction by observing the contrails. If they shred sideways, the wind at their level is directed across them. If they do not shred and instead intensify by growing small turret-like tops along their length, then the upper wind is running along the trail.

If the contrail and surface winds are both blowing in the same direction and the contrail is also growing turrets (use your binoculars to get a good look), you can anticipate no great change in the weather for several hours. If the upper wind is backed to the surface wind, you can probably expect an anticyclone (high pressure system) and quiet sailing days, and vice versa.

In temperate latitudes of the Northern Hemisphere, if you stand with your back to the surface wind and cirrus clouds or contrails move from your left hand, then a warm front or occlusion is on the way and the weather will deteriorate; near or full gale is likely. In the Southern Hemisphere, stand facing the wind. This test may give as much as 18 to 24 hours warning.

If there is a ridge of high pressure and the wind is from a westerly point and blowing less than 11 to 16 knots, watch for any sign of it backing toward the south. If it does and there are thick contrails and/or ice clouds high in the sky, you have two clues to what is coming. First, a backing (shifting counterclockwise) wind should always be suspected, because winds usually back ahead of coming fronts and troughs. Second, the density of the trails or high clouds reveals plenty of water vapor aloft which goes with a vigorous front that is coming.

The buildup of *cumulus* clouds (detached, generally dense, with sharp outlines) can lead, especially in the trade wind belts, to the giant *cumulonimbus*—the anvil-shaped thunderheads which may signify squall activity.

Squalls may be localized, part of a frontal system, or associated with a major storm system such as a hurricane. Few areas of the world's oceans are free of squalls, so be prepared to meet one anytime while sailing offshore or even while daysailing.

Squalls usually give enough warning to allow you to either avoid them or prepare for them. A squall that precedes a cold front, for instance, shows itself as a long line of rolling, menacing clouds that may contain sudden heavy winds, rain, thunder, and lightning. Advancing across the horizon, the squall looks dangerous; once it is spotted, sails should come down and the boat be put in a readiness condition, with compass course plotted and the boat's position accounted for. Once the squall hits, visibility will be reduced to nil until the front passes through.

You can avoid being caught unprepared for a local squall by taking frequent bearings on it. If the bearings do not change, you are on a collision course with it. If your bearing diminishes, the squall will pass in front of you. And if the bearing increases, you are passing in front of the squall.

WIND

The velocity of the wind in any area depends upon the pressure there, or more strictly the pressure differential between it and the adjacent areas. Wind pressure increases as the square of its velocity. Turbulence, especially around high land, can generate gusts 40 percent higher than average wind. A meteorologist records the pressure distribution by what are termed isobars, which are lines on a weather map joining points of equal atmospheric pressure.

The closer the spacing of the isobars the greater the differential in pressure, since the same difference in pressure exists over a shorter distance of sea. Knowing this is important in reading a weather map. The closer the isobars, the stronger the wind represented by them. An increase in wind velocity is experienced as the low-pressure center is approached, until the zone is reached where the air begins to turn upwards. The alignment of the isobars is that of the wind occurring some 2,000 feet from the sea surface, essentially at a level beyond the frictional effect of the earth's surface. This is known as the geostrophic wind.

Wind speeds as forecast do not allow for the local shape of shoreline, and particularly for wind actions like funneling and canalization. The wind will follow a waterway whenever it can because even the choppiest sea surface is smooth compared to the land, and air always takes the line of least resistance.

If a deep low exists over the land with isobars for strong wind roughly paralleling the coastline, the coast can channel the wind along the shore and increases its speed by perhaps as much as two Beaufort notations (see page 118). This phenomenon illustrates the important point that gales are not uniform in strength over a given area, and that wind forces can thus be much higher locally. It applies particularly when in the vicinity of land, where violent squalls and gusts can funnel down valleys.

Thirty-three feet aloft is the correct position for judging wind on the Beaufort scale. One third should be added to the wind speed recorded by the anemometer used in the cockpit to equate to Beaufort notation.

Be alert to unusual local winds. Southern California's Santa Ana wind, for instance, can attain velocities of 60 to 70 knots from the northeast. The wind strikes suddenly and is characterized by dry air, absence of low clouds and fog, and no dew. The smog from the inland cities can be seen as a dull brown haze spreading seaward. The wind appears as a rapidly advancing dark blue line on the horizon.

Remember too that when the mean wind speed is 25 knots, the average speed of gusts is between 33 and 41 knots; and maximum gust speed is between 40 and 50 knots. But gusts that come off of the land can be much higher than the mean wind speed. At sea, big wind gusts come down from thousands of feet aloft, where the wind is stronger, and these descending winds often bring rain or hail. They may sweep across you every 20 minutes or so, bringing gusts 10–15 knots stronger than the mean. Open sea conditions with a fetch of over five miles will produce less variation in gust speeds but still may have considerable influence.

Yachts are most commonly caught in storms and hurricanes on the western side of the Atlantic from June to November, and principally in September, between New England and Bermuda, Florida, and the Caribbean. Tropical storms have a mean wind force of 34–63 knots. Hurricanes have a mean wind force of 64 knots or more, with wind raging as high as 170 knots. The maximum wind velocity in a hurricane is not known, as most anemometers stop working at about 125 knots.

In these hurricanes, waves of 35–40 feet are not uncommon, and in giant storms, they can reach an incredible 45–50 feet.

WAVES AND WAVE ACTION

Waves can show the sailor the direction and speed of the wind, warn him of approaching storms, and indicate shallow water and currents.

Wind of consistent force tends to produce a water surface of consistent appearance. In 1805, the British admiral Sir Francis Beaufort compiled a table of the appearances and forces of waves from which he developed the Beaufort Scale, with wind velocities added to forces. (See page 118.)

It is not always possible to judge the state of the sea from the Beaufort notation, however, even in the open ocean. Wave size may be increased by a long duration of wind and unlimited fetch. Or a confused wave pattern may result from a shift of wind, frontal gusts, or a

Beaufort Wind Scale

Beaufort Number or Force	Wind Speed			World Meteorological Organization Description
	Knots	mph	km/hr	
0	under 1	under 1	under 1	Calm
1	1–3	1–3	1–5	Light Air
2	4–6	4–7	6–11	Light Breeze
3	7–10	8–12	12–19	Gentle Breeze
4	11–16	13–18	20–28	Moderate Breeze
5	17–21	19–24	29–38	Fresh Breeze
6	22–27	25–31	39–49	Strong Breeze
7	28–33	32–38	50–61	Near Gale
8	34–40	39–46	62–74	Gale
9	41–47	47–54	75–88	Strong Gale
10	48–55	55–63	89–102	Storm
11	56–63	64–72	103–117	Violent Storm
12	64 and over	73 and over	118 and over	Hurricane

Estimating Wind Speed		
Effects Observed at Sea	Effects Observed near Land	Effects Observed on Land
Sea like a mirror	Calm	Calm; smoke rises vertically
Ripples with appearance of scales; no foam crests	Small sailboat just has steerage way	Smoke drift indicates wind direction; vanes do not move
Small wavelets; crests of glassy appearance, not breaking	Wind fills the sails of small boats which then travel at about 1–2 knots	Wind felt on face; leaves rustle; vanes begin to move
Large wavelets; crests begin to break, scattered whitecaps	Sailboats begin to heel and travel at about 3–4 knots	Leaves, small twigs in constant motion; light flags extended
Small waves 0.5–1.25 meters high, becoming longer; numerous whitecaps	Good working breeze, sailboats carry all sail with good heel	Dust, leaves, and loose paper raised up; small branches move
Moderate waves of 1.25–2.5 meters taking longer form; many whitecaps; some spray	Sailboats shorten sail	Small trees in leaf begin to sway
Larger waves 2.5–4 meters forming; whitecaps everywhere; more spray	Sailboats have double reefed mainsails	Larger branches of trees in motion; whistling heard in wires
Sea heaps up, waves 4–6 meters; white foam from breaking waves begins to be blown in streaks	Boats remain in harbor; those at sea heave-to	Whole trees in motion; resistance felt in walking against wind
Moderately high (4–6 meters) waves of greater length; edges of crests begin to break into spindrift; foam is blown in well-marked streaks	All boats make for harbor, if near	Twigs and small branches broken off trees; progress generally impaired
High waves (6 meters); sea begins to roll; dense streaks of foam; spray may reduce visibility		Slight structural damage occurs; slate blown from roofs
Very high waves (6–9 meters) with overhanging crests; sea takes a white appearance as foam is blown in very dense streaks; rolling is heavy and visibility is reduced		Seldom experienced on land; trees broken or uprooted; considerable structural damage occurs
Exceptionally high (9–14 meters) waves; sea covered with white foam patches; visibility still more reduced		Very rarely experienced on land; usually accompanied by widespread damage
Air filled with foam; waves over 14 meters; sea completely white with driving spray; visibility greatly reduced		

combination of wave trains caused by the movements of depressions.

The proper term for waves formed by the winds in a local area is "seas." After they leave a storm area, waves change shape and become "swells." Swells travel ("fetch") until they reach land, possibly thousands of miles away, and tend to get longer, lower, and more regular as they travel.

For a wind of a certain speed, blowing a long time over a long distance, seas of a certain range of heights will form. Eventually, even if the wind blows for a longer time or over a greater distance, the seas will become no rougher. Only an increase in wind speed will increase the height of the seas.

By their nature, seas are highly irregular. They do not all travel in exactly the same direction. Winds stack up waves with widely varying lengths and heights, and as the waves travel they combine and cancel one another continually.

The most important characteristic of seas is their unpredictability. You cannot count on finding a trough at a regular distance behind a crest. When peaks meet, the waves add to one another. When a peak meets a trough, they cancel one another. The highest seas form quickly as two waves join.

When the wind speed picks up and becomes more gusty, the waves almost immediately show increased height. Likewise the two decline together.

As wind begins to blow across a calm surface, the first response on the water is capillary waves of high frequency—tiny surface ripples that form a regular diamond-shaped pattern. If the wind continues to blow and the capillary waves reach a wave length of about three quarters of an inch (1.73 cm) and a speed of about nine inches (24 cm) per second they are called gravity waves. The major difference in capillary and gravity waves is their durability. If the wind were to die the tiny capillary waves would quickly disappear but the larger

gravity waves would carry on until they fetched up against something.

When judging wind direction from waves you should know that the little wavelets formed by the wind go more or less downwind. The actual waves may vary by 20 degrees or more from the wind direction. Looking straight upwind, streaks from strong winds seem to converge at the horizon. Looking downwind, trails in foam left by breaking waves appear to run straight. Use the wind direction and direction changes as part of the weather data you've collected to predict the weather in the area of your boat.

Winds that are important in ocean wave generation are those produced in low-pressure centers, or cyclones. High-pressure systems, or anti-cyclones, contain very mild

Crew members should have foul-weather gear suitable for all conditions and should wear a harness at all times on deck.
Gary Jobson

winds and are important mainly in separating the cyclonic centers from calm weather. These latter envelop large tracts of ocean and land masses, whereas cyclones are concentrated over much smaller zones, although their centers move more rapidly than the ill-defined high pressure regions.

The height of waves is often overstated by sailors and indeed sometimes by professionals. When the estimate is compared with the sea disturbance scale, taking into account wind force, duration, and fetch, it will often be found that the height of the waves cannot possibly be what they appear. (Wave height is the distance from trough to crest.)

To sailors envisioning catastrophic events, the most critical factor is actually not wave height but rather wave slope. Constant steep seas induce stress forces—gear-busting conditions that can wreck a yacht. In gale force weather or worse, surfing down a steep wave slope can result in pitchpoling if the vessel isn't slowed down to five knots or less. Lying beam to in steep waves can end up in a knockdown or capsize. Knowing exactly what wind and wave conditions you *are* seeing can play a major role in the safety of your boat.

Knowing what causes wave height changes in the first place can be helpful too. When waves come into shallow water they tend to slow down, increase in height, and be bent or refracted. Along a coastline the inshore ends of waves turn to become nearly parallel to the coast.

The first warning of shallow water may be the boat's wake building up off the stem quarter. A tall wave cannot live in shallow water; increasing friction against the bottom eventually causes it to break down. For example, a sea may be choppy in ten feet of water but broken down to smooth in two feet.

When waves strike vertical surfaces, they do not break but are reflected and interact with incoming waves to make a very confused sea. For just that reason it is not a good idea to anchor near a bulkhead.

Currents affect both seas and swells. Current moving opposite to the waves will slow them down and make them steeper. Current moving with the waves will make them be longer and have more rounded crests; a strong one can nearly flatten a sea. Note that a current may be less at the edges of an inlet having a deep-draft ship channel, because the greater volume of water must move faster. And if a current is moving at right angles to the waves it will not have much effect on them.

Strong tidal streams will of course add to or reduce the strength of the wind appreciably, depending on direction. In addition, the stream causes an increase in the wave height and steepness when it is running against waves or wind, or a decrease when it is running with them.

Knowledge of these interactions of wind and waves is vital to both offshore and coastal sailors. Unstable seas, and therefore potentially dangerous ones, can occur with the veer of the wind when a cold front passes through, accompanied by violent squalls of possibly 50 knots or more that form new trains of waves across the existing run of seas. However, the torrential rains that may accompany violent squalls or gales can flatten big seas.

During gales, check the bottom near your boat. Areas where there is irregularity on the bottom, or rock ledges, even if deep down, can cause seas to break and can be nearly as dangerous as lee shores. A ship's wake crossing the big seas running in a storm may also cause the waves to break.

Freak waves created in all those unstable conditions may attain dimensions dangerous to small yachts at Force 8 (34–40 knots mean) and even lower. Of the waves in the 1979 Fastnet the well-known oceanographer Willard J. Pierson wrote: "It always continues to amaze me that seafaring men are not aware that in a storm such as that which occurred during the 1979 Fastnet Race, a freak wave *must* happen sometime. In any wave system, after a long enough time, an exceptionally high wave

"A great wall of water was towering above her."

will occur. These monstrous, oversized waves are improbable but still possible. Hence, they do happen. They can happen at any time, and the exact time of occurrence of such an outsized wave can never be predicted."

Freak waves do indeed happen. Phil Weld, once hove-to offshore in his trimaran *Gulfstreamer* during an Atlantic storm, had no warning of the approach of a rogue wave that capsized his vessel; the boat stayed afloat upside down for three days until he and his crew were rescued.

One of the most famous of all rogue waves hit the yacht *Tzu Hang* in the Southern Ocean. As described by Miles Smeeton in *Once Is Enough* (Adlard Coles, Ltd.):

"A wave passed under *Tzu Hang* and she slewed slightly. Beryl corrected her easily and when she was down in the hollow, she looked off to check her align-

124 Storm Sailing

ment. Close behind her a great wall of water was towering above her, so wide that she couldn't see its flanks, so high and so steep that she knew *Tzu Hang* could not ride over it. It didn't seem to be breaking as the other waves had broken but water was cascading down its front like a waterfall."

The wall of water swept away both masts and the doghouse, leaving a half-swamped boat with a six-foot opening where the coach roof had been. That the crew of *Tzu Hang* was able to jury rig the vessel and limp to safety is one of the miracles of modern seamanship.

Wind and wave action during a hurricane assault was described by one yachtsman as follows: "Waves were collapsing on top of waves, that were collapsing on top of waves, that were collapsing on top of waves. Everything was gray and white and screaming. Waves struck the boat from 360 degrees. The noise of the wind had gone beyond loudness. It was simply a dull white sound."

And another yachtsman gave the following description of a rogue wave: "The gale was blowing as hard as ever, but there we were in our snug, dry little cabin with an oil lamp burning as it was dusk, almost dark, in fact. It came with devastating suddenness; a great fiend of a sea that picked the yacht up, threw her over on her port side and then burst over her. There was an awful splintering of wood, a crash of broken glass and in came a roaring cataract of water."

JURY RIGS

Modern rigs are light. If raced and sailed hard they undergo tremendous loads, especially in heavy wind and seas. The possibility of a dismasting is always present and for this reason skipper and crew should be prepared with tools and resourceful planning in case an emergency does take place.

For me, dismasting has happened several times—on the Twelve-Meter yachts *Defender* and *Courageous*, on a

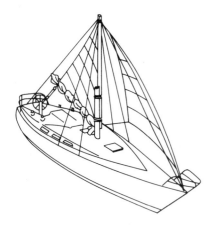

28-foot catboat, *Bat,* and on several smaller racing dinghies. In each case the spar failed because of a faulty piece of rigging or mast gear and went over the side. The broken mast section was cut away to prevent damage to the hull and saved. On the Twelves, of course, we were towed back to our dock, but if the accidents had happened offshore the emphasis would have been on setting up some kind of temporary jury rig to get the boat back to port. Even in closed-circuit racing, teams are urged to finish, even under jury rig. The Intercollegiate Yacht Racing Association of North America actively encourages crews to act in a seamanlike fashion and try to finish the race.

Rigging failure seems to bring out the competitive spirit in good skippers to get home despite the odds. At the 1975 St. Petersburg Olympic Training Regatta I was sailing with Olympic Bronze Medalist Don Cohan in a Flying Dutchman. On a particularly windy day the top of our mast snapped off and made sailing under the main impossible. Although there were a number of rescue boats in the vicinity Don insisted that we make it back to the dock on our own—a three-mile sail. So with jury-rigged jib and no mainsail we limped back to St. Petersburg. There was no way Cohan would allow himself to be towed in.

In 1965, a particularly strong southeasterly blow hit Barnegat Bay, N.J., during a race of 22 E-Scows. Only four finished—including Runyan Colie, who had broken his mast with a three-mile downwind run to go. His solution had been to jury rig a spinnaker pole, and using a small reaching sail he had drifted downwind at about five knots and finished the race, completing the points he needed to win the season's championship.

Stories of jury rigging at sea among cruising vessels and singlehanders are more common than is realized. The crew of *Tzu Hang* not only rigged a means of continuing to sail but also found a way of covering the cabin area after the coachroof had been destroyed. Angus Primrose's 33-foot sloop was dismasted during the 1976

Observer Singlehanded Transatlantic Race. Under jury rig he returned to England. (Ironically he made the same passage again successfully in 1980, but was lost at sea several months later in a coastal storm off South Carolina.)

Probably the most recent successful attempt at keeping a boat going under jury rig occurred in the 1981–82 Whitbread Around the World Race, when the 68-foot yacht *Ceramco New Zealand* was dismasted off the coast of Africa. With a course fair for Capetown in sunlit tropical seas and a 25-knot breeze, the 80-foot spar let go, crumpling over the starboard rail as a shroud gave way. Fortunately the weather was good, and within 30 hours the seasoned crew under the direction of skipper Peter Blake had the boat going with some speed again.

Jay Broze and Simon Gundry, writing in *Sail* (January 1982) provided the details of the jury rig:

"The intact 50-foot top section of the spar was on deck as were the tangled rigging, snapped shroud, and salty sails. They (the crew) also managed to get the #6 genoa lashed to the 15-foot stump of the mast that remained above the deck . . .

"The spar was trimmed at the break, and the cook's breadboard reinforced with odd lots of genoa track, was positioned in front of the stump. This would be the (mast) step. The inboard mounts for the top spreaders were at the very bottom of the mast section and they were used to attach positioning tackle to both rails in order to keep the butt of the spar centered. The tall (spar) section was then hung out over the bow with two men sitting on the inboard end to keep it from teetering off.

"The mast was raised using the stump as a gin pole. The crew passed a line over the stump and back to a grinder, with a second lifting point closer to the base, and started cranking. The positioning tackle and the new shrouds were winched taut to keep the spar under control, and although it nearly escaped once, they had it wire-strapped to the stump before midday and at noon

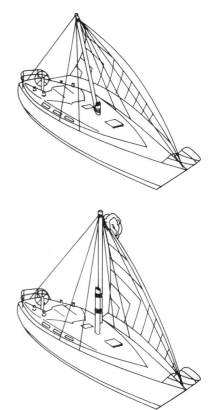

Figure 17: *Some methods of jury-rigging masts.*

they were flying a little genoa off the masthead. The day ended with *Ceramco* sliding south under a main reefed down to the fourth point and a double headsail rig, making over eight knots.

"Since there was no way to lower the main (it had to be lashed to the spar), the provision for reefing in a real gale was a series of brailing lines that would bundle it up the mast. There were no surviving bits of rod short enough to use for standing rigging, so former running backstays found their way from the masthead to the deck and back to a winch or stopper. In fact, the deck was crisscrossed with drum-tight standing rigging."

By this means (plus a bipole mizzen mast using two spinnaker poles) *Ceramco* sailed 4,000 miles in 24 days from the point of her dismasting to Capetown. It was apparent, as was pointed out, that *Ceramco* got as far as she did because she was loaded with gear—plus the tools to manufacture new rigs out of the remains of the old.

In dealing with dismastings and rigging failure, having the proper tools on board becomes very important. At the very least carry a pair of heavy wire cutters and a carbon-toothed/hacksaw and spare blades. Some vessels carry a portable battery-operated saw. A swaging

Aboard Ceramco New Zealand, *the crew cleans up the results of dismasting, clearing away shrouds and other rigging. In jury rigging a new mast, which was lashed to the stump of the old one, a bread-board was used as a mast base. Note details of block and tackle arrangement used to hold the mast in place.*
Geoff Stagg

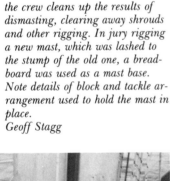

tool is useful and anyone planning to be at sea for any length of time should have stainless steel replacement rigging wire, and plenty of spare blocks, shackles, and line. If the mast goes over the side, it must be cut away to avoid damaging the hull, but if it can then be hauled back on board, one should do so to provide a makeshift spar. In heavy weather, of course, this may be impossible.

In my experience there are certain patterns to dismastings. The mast goes because of a failure in the rigging and it usually happens during maneuvering or when the mainsail is flogging intensely. This was the case with the Twelve-Meter *Defender* during practice in September 1982. We had just started a race. The Mylar/Kevlar mainsail was not trimmed in hard but was luffing violently in a 25-knot breeze. Perhaps the shaking of the top of the mast caused the upper spreader to pull apart; the mast collapsed in two pieces.

There are several ways of preventing dismasting, one of which should take place at sea, the others on shore. At sea, avoid shock loading if you possibly can because it puts extraordinary strains on the rigging. Shock loading occurs when all of the pressure of wind and sea is placed on one spot of the boat. Trimming the main in, for instance, gives the mast extra support. When the main luffs, the backstay undergoes a great deal of stress. It's natural for spars to move while the boat is underway. Like an airplane wing, the strength of the spar is in its flexibility. Still, precautions should be taken while maneuvering.

Other precautions to prevent rigging collapse should be taken on shore. While race-boat owners have the wherewithal to x-ray tangs, fittings, and standing rigging before major races, the average skipper may not be able to do this. Still, all rigging should be checked every season by a master rigger and replacements made where necessary. Anyone planning a major ocean passage should check every piece of rigging before leaving, down to shackles, turnbuckles, and cotter pins.

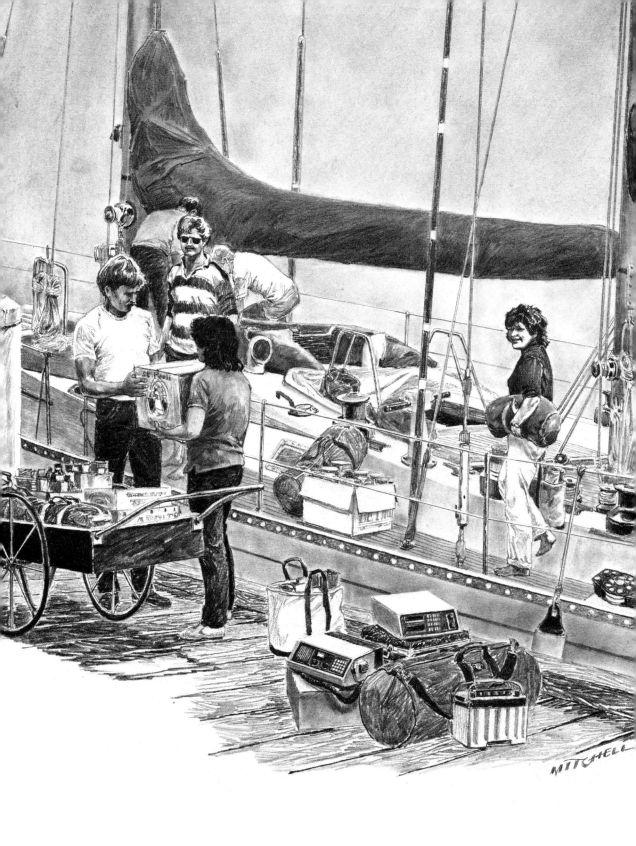

Heavy weather sailing places enormous stress on boats and gear. The competent skipper knows how green water and gale force winds can punish a vessel that would otherwise be trouble free in normal sailing. Offshore racing organizations know this as well, and their rules and recommendations for required safety equipment have been reinforced over the years as new storm experiences come to light. Gear must be preserved for use in an emergency. Here are some thoughts on what to carry against the presumption of bad weather—and how to take care of it.

CHAPTER 6

Equipment — The Care and Feeding of Essential Gear

DECK GEAR

Winches, too often, are considered part of the boat's furniture instead of vital tools that must be ready to work instantly. The bigger the boat the more important the winching machinery, because it provides nearly all the mechanical advantage on board.

Winches, therefore, must be kept functioning at their most efficient levels—mainly by guarding against interior corrosion from salt spray and dirt. They should be washed with fresh water whenever the vessel is in port and should be broken down, checked for malfunctioning parts, and cleaned and greased each month. Every winch is supplied with a maintenance manual and in most cases the job can be "cookbooked"—just follow the manual's steps.

If your manual doesn't list steps, here is a general procedure to follow: The drum should be taken off and oil squirted on the pawls. Do not use synthetic lubricant because it often conducts electricity and may cause electrolysis between dissimilar metals in the winch, causing the drum to seize up. When you take the winch apart, check for salt deposits on the bearings and clean them carefully if salt is present. Crank the winch in both directions and check to see that everything is rotating freely and smoothly with the drum off. After you've cleaned the bearings with kerosene, wipe them off before regreasing. Use a product recommended by the manufacturer.

If the winch is not working, the pawls may be the problem. If you do any heavy racing or cruising, I recommend that several pawls of sufficient size and shape as well as pawl springs be carried in the boat's spare parts kit.

Halyard winches are best kept off the mast. The thin walls of the spar may not be able to withstand the heavy loading.
Peter Thompson
Gary Jobson

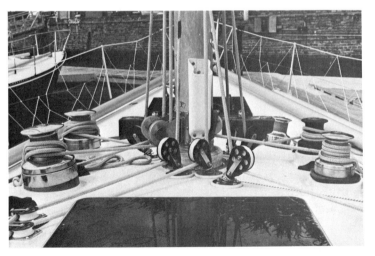

When storing a boat between sailing seasons you don't really need winch covers, although some skippers cover black anodized winches in port and between seasons. If you do so, make sure that the covers are made of canvas and not vinyl, so that air can get to the winches and prevent moisture from being trapped.

SAFETY EQUIPMENT

New revised rules of the Ocean Racing Club (see Appendix A) spell out quite clearly what most racing yachts are required to carry. Yours may be a cruising boat, but even so, the regulations can serve as a guide for any cruising vessel planning to go offshore. Heavy storms treat racing and cruising boats alike.

The requirements include:

- *Heaving line* 50 feet, ready and accessible from the cockpit.
- *Wooden plugs* Soft, of varying shapes and sizes to plug through-hull fittings.
- *Anti-capsize security* Internal ballast must be securely fastened in position. So must batteries, stove, gas bottles, tanks and engines, outboard motors, anchors and chains.
- *Hatch covers* Must be capable of being secured in position and tethered to the yacht by a lanyard or other mechanical means, to prevent them from being lost overboard.
- *Buckets* Two of "stout construction" with at least nine liters capacity, with lanyard.
- *Flashlights* One suitable for signaling, several extras, water-resistant, with spare batteries and bulbs.
- *First-aid kit* With medical manual.
- *Foghorn*
- *Radar reflector*

- *International code flags and International code book* For larger offshore yachts.

- *Fire extinguishers* Readily accessible and of the type and number required by the country of registry.

- *Tools and spare parts* Including bolt and cable cutters, and other means for disconnecting or severing the standing rigging from the hull, in the case of dismasting.

- *Anchors* Two anchors with cables, which must be securely fastened in the position recorded on the Rating Certificate when not in use. Yachts rating under 21 feet must carry one anchor and cable.

- *Lifelines (jackstays)* Should be run up the center or both sides of the deck from bow to stern so the crew can walk the full length of the deck without unhooking safety harnesses. Rig at least a ¼-inch wire with a terminal at each end to deck pad eyes. Also locate a number of pad eyes in the cockpit so individual crewmen can hook into them.

- *Handholds* Should be strong and big enough to get one's whole hand around and should be available throughout the interior of the boat.

STEERING GEAR

Crewman Robert Symonette, who as I've mentioned is an experienced offshore sailor and transatlantic racer, wrote me after the 1979 Fastnet: "In looking back at the Fastnet, one of the "must-do's" was to check frequently for the possibility of steering failure. . . . Having had steering gear failures on *Caribbee*, *Figaro*, and *Finisterre*, and various transatlantic and other races, I know it's something that has to be watched. Failure can take place in a turning block, a wire jumping the quadrant, or the bicycle chain up through the pedestal to the sprocket at the wheel. Once again, we tried for prevention by observation."

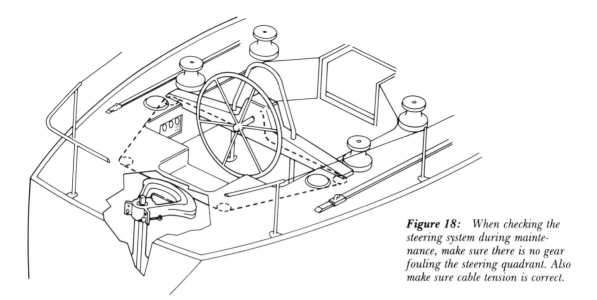

Figure 18: *When checking the steering system during maintenance, make sure there is no gear fouling the steering quadrant. Also make sure cable tension is correct.*

It is precisely to prevent this disastrous sort of failure that the steering system should receive frequent maintenance and checking. Fish hooks, flat spots, or chafed wire in the wire cable, especially in areas of constant sheave contact, often appear with just normal wear and tear. Metallic dust or shavings indicate that there are sheave alignment problems or excessive bushing wear. Grease or oil any squeaky areas well. If there is any chain rust, clean and oil the chain. Check the wheel sprocket and lubricate it, if necessary. If there is rod linkage between the wheel and the shaft, check it for wear, lubricate it, and try to remove any slop in the system. Finally, get out the emergency tiller and make sure it can be put to work quickly.

The Offshore Racing Council requires that all yachts carry an emergency tiller capable of being fitted to the rudder stock. Crews (according to the ORC) must also be aware of alternative methods of steering the yacht in the event of total rudder failure in any sea condition.

The crew of your yacht should practice installing and operating the emergency steering system under your direction. Devise a series of logical steps for installing the spare tiller, and work out whether a block and tackle or winch system is required to operate the unit. Emergency tillers are often so short and heavy that they lack sufficient leverage to steer a boat adequately. In such cases a small block and tackle system and two nearby winches can often provide the necessary mechanical advantage to control the boat safely hour after hour.

Emergency tillers should not be constructed of ferrous metal that can affect the compass. A two-part emergency tiller is easier to stow and easier to install, and can also offer increased leverage over a one-piece model that is made short for stowage purposes.

If there is no emergency tiller, or it doesn't work, a fairly simple steering system can be made by putting a hole in the top of the trailing edge of the rudder blade. In an emergency you can pass a line through the hole and use the line to steer with (with the aid of winches, of course).

SAFETY HARNESSES AND PFDs

The safety harness did not come into general use until the 1950 Transatlantic Race. There are still those who think that safety at sea depends primarily on self-reliance and that a safety harness is only a secondary aid that should not be overused. However, the worthwhile use of the harness is well documented beginning in the 1970 Bermuda Race, when several men on *Scylla* went overboard, but were wearing safety harnesses and were recovered. Such near misses from disaster serve as a reminder that in a gale even when all seems under control, there is always the chance of an exceptional gust of wind or a freak wave, or both at the same time, that may knock a boat flat on her beam ends and sweep the crew overboard. Most often the danger of losing a person overboard is greatest when the safety harness is temporarily disengaged, either when coming on deck or changing helmsmen.

The 1979 Fastnet inquiry went into the uses of harnesses during the storm very thoroughly and came up with the following comments—the need for double harnesses in severe conditions, the danger of clipping onto outboard lifelines rather than to inboard safety lines from the cockpit to points forward, the advantage of having permanent lines anchored in danger areas of the deck so that crew can clip in, and the practical advantages of a combination harness/lifejacket.

Some rules about harnesses:

• You cannot foresee the conditions for a watch when you come up on deck. Therefore, always bring a harness with you when you are on watch and stow it within reach. Put it on when the weather deteriorates and always wear it at night.

• Check all harnesses periodically to see that the carabinier hooks work easily without sticking, that the webbing is sound, that there are no frayed stitches, and that the line leading from harness to clip hook is of webbing that is at least one inch wide. Practice wearing the harness under mild conditions. Practice reefing, changing sails, and moving about on deck with it.

• When a storm is about to enfold the yacht, the skipper is responsible for warning the crew to clip on to something secure immediately upon going on deck. Pick a strong point—a pad eye, binnacle brace, or a genoa track slider.

• Some crew members prefer to have a short line on their harness to prevent being swept overboard. The disadvantage to a short line, however, is the need to rehook frequently.

• In extreme weather, take the precaution of using the harness with a second safety line so that there is no possibility of being thrown overboard while the harness is being rehooked.

Equipment   **137**

• At the outset of bad weather, rig lines crisscrossing the cockpit so that if the boat is knocked down, none of the crew has far to go before grabbing a line to keep from going over the side.

Life jackets (personal flotation devices, or PFDs) are another known lifesaver. The U.S. Coast Guard requires that there be an approved one on board for each member of the crew, plus one throwable device. The Offshore Racing Council is equally strict in adhering to the same rule, and in addition requires that the life jackets have whistles attached to them.

Other ORC rules for safety devices insist that even yachts racing in short events close to shore (Category 4) must have at least one horseshoe-type life ring equipped with a waterproof light and a drogue, kept within reach of the helmsman and ready for instant use. Yachts in more extended races near shore must have at least one horseshoe-type life ring equipped with a drogue and self-igniting light (reversible strobe) with a duration of at least 45 minutes, also kept within reach of the helmsman and ready for use. Yachts participating in offshore races (Category 1) should have at least one horseshoe life ring equipped with a whistle, dye marker, drogue, a self-igniting high intensity water light (strobe) and a pole and flag. The pole is to be attached to the ring with 25 feet (8 m) of floating line and is to be of a length and so ballasted that the flag will fly at least eight feet (2.45 m) off the water.

The 1979 Fastnet Race Inquiry recommended that personal flotation devices have collar-retaining straps and, in the case of inflatable jackets, pressure relief valves. It also recommended that discussions be conducted with manufacturers of harnesses and life jackets concerning wider production of combined safety harnesses and life jackets.

Only ninety-one percent of the boats in the Fastnet fleet were equipped with life jackets; 43 percent reported that life jackets were worn during the storm and

53 percent that they were not worn; 39 percent reported that life jackets impaired working efficiency and 39 percent that they did not. In general, crews appeared to attach considerably less importance to life jackets than to safety harnesses as items of safety equipment.

It is very important that all your PFDs be cared for and stowed properly if they are to continue to provide the proper amount of buoyancy when needed. Check them regularly against punctures, or deterioration because of sunlight, mildew, humidity, and abrasion.

LIFE RAFTS

Ocean racing rules are very strict, as well they should be, on the question of life rafts. There are no rules other than prudence for cruising boats, but cruising skippers should nevertheless outfit their boats with at least the following minimum racing requirements. The ORC states that yachts in the top three racing categories (see Appendix A) have rafts on board that carry the entire crew. Each raft must:

Be carried on deck (not under a dinghy) or in special stowage opening immediately to the deck, that contains life raft(s) only.

Be designed and used solely for saving life at sea.

Have at least two separate buoyancy compartments, each of which is automatically inflatable; and be capable of carrying its rated capacity with one compartment deflated.

Have a canopy to cover the occupants.

Have been inspected, tested, and approved within one year by the manufacturer or other competent authority.

Carry the following equipment appropriately secured: bellows, pump, or other means for maintaining inflation of the air chambers; signaling light; three hand flares; bailer; repair kit; two paddles; knife; and (for boats in Category 1—extended offshore racing) emergency water and food.

The requirements for gear to be contained in the raft is recognizably minimum. Rafts should also carry EPIRB transmitters; their value in saving lives has been proven. In addition to extra flares and other visual communication devices (mirrors) inside the raft, there should also be stowed as close to the raft as possible a kit containing fishing equipment, navigation gear, hand compass, charts, a first-aid kit and manual, additional warm clothes, a hat, sunscreen, desalinization devices, and emergency rations.

The reason for the annual inspection of the life raft is to be sure that it will inflate and stay inflated and support you and your crew with fresh gear and provisions. The inspection also allows you to see inside the raft, check the equipment, and modify gear as needed.

There are three types of marine life rafts. The open raft keeps you afloat and protects you from some thermal loss to the ocean. The canopy on a canopy raft is supported by an inflatable chamber and offers protection from the sun, wind, and rain. It also helps to reduce loss of body fluids because you are shaded. The third type of raft is a canopy raft that has water ballast underneath it for stability. The ballasted raft has the advantage of offering greater stability, especially in high, steep seas. The ballast is provided by a bag that resembles the canopy but is on the underside of the raft and is filled with water.

All three types of marine rafts should have buoyancy chambers, each one capable of supporting the rated number of people above the water. Allowance is only four square feet per person. Those in the raft are counted on to act as the ballast unless the raft is ballasted in itself.

STORM SAILS

Offshore racing yachts cannot participate in deep-water events unless they carry the prerequisite number of storm sails. The required inventory again sets a pat-

tern for the cruising yacht—as do the attendant rigging requirements:

• *One storm trysail* not larger than 0.175 P × E in area. It shall be sheeted independently of the boom and shall have neither a headboard nor battens and be of a cloth weight greater than that of the mainsail.

• *One storm jib* of not more than 0.05 IG^2 in area, the luff of which does not exceed 0.65 IG, and of suitable strength for the purpose.

• *One heavy-weather jib* of cloth weight heavier than that of the mainsail with an area not greater than 0.135 IG^2 and which does not contain reef points.

• *One heavy-weather jib* as in above, or heavy-weather sail in the boat with no forestay, and reefing equipment for the mainsail (Categories 3 and 4).

"A life raft should carry extra flares and other visual communications devices."

Equipment **141**

• *Any storm or heavy-weather jib* if designed for a sea-stay or luff-groove device shall have an alternative method of attachment to the stay or a wire luff (all categories).

• No mast shall have less than two halyards, each capable of hoisting a sail (all categories).

With the proper storm sail inventory on board, practice using each of the sails, first on a light day, then in at least 25 to 30 knots of wind. Remember, all maneuvers in storm conditions—moving sail bags, hanging on, raising and sheeting sails—are more difficult in strong winds and waves and are aggravated by fatigue, seasickness, and fear.

Label everything: corners of the sail (head, tack, and clew), leads, and halyard positions. Tie sheets to clews individually in case one should break. Do not use shackles, as they can shake off and are dangerous to crew. Use a bowline instead. And keep a spare halyard available.

In over 35 knots of wind use a heavy-weather jib, roughly the size of a #4 genoa. It should not have reef points because a wave could land in the reefed section of the foot and tear out the reef. With a grooved headstay you need an alternate means to attach the jib. This is commonly a row of grommets behind the luff tape used to tie or lace the sail to the headstay.

In over 50 knots of wind you need a small storm jib of very strong material. It can be set on the headstay but is better on an intermediate forestay. This will reduce lee helm and keep crew off the bow of the boat.

A storm trysail has an area less than a third that of the mainsail, and no headboards or battens because they could break or chafe in storm conditions. The storm trysail should be easily set from deck level, and must sheet to a block on the rail or deck and not to the end of the boom. (See page 61.) The boom should be lashed to the leeward deck for safety.

MAN OVERBOARD

One of the most fearsome accidents that happens at sea is losing a crewman overboard. Procedures for recovery, however, are clear cut, and have resulted in rescues time after time. Every crew putting to sea should be familiar with the methods of man-overboard recovery and must make every effort to drill regularly.

Man overboard procedures begin with prevention. The skipper and watch captains should keep the crew alert, enforce the harness rule, be sure all rigging (running backstays, etc.) is made up securely to provide handholds.

In a man-overboard situation, the actions of the crew are actually more important than the efficiency of the lifesaving apparatus. The first steps are to mark the victim's position *immediately* by throwing him something that floats him—assign a single crew member the sole task of watching him—and to get the vessel under control for maneuvering to pick him up. There should be a standard plan for each of these steps—a quick, precise

CHAPTER 7

Safety and Emergency Procedures

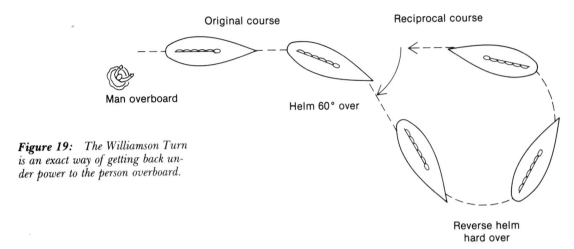

Original course   Reciprocal course

Man overboard

Helm 60° over

Reverse helm
hard over

Figure 19: *The Williamson Turn is an exact way of getting back under power to the person overboard.*

return that covers all points of sailing and all possible sail and crew combinations that apply to your boat, as well as a plan to facilitate the pickup, with each crew member assigned to a certain task (see Figure 20, page 148). Keep track of the precise time, average speed, and average course on which the boat is heading away from the person in the water. If you are under sail, approach the victim with the wind abeam so that you have control over both boat speed and course. Drop the headsail when you are within 100 yards of the target area so that you have visibility and continued control over the boat's speed. Ease the main boom out to the rigging and rig a foreguy to hold it there. When you have reached the person in the water, put the wheel hard up or the tiller hard down and fix it there. The boat will now tend itself without help from the crew.

If you are sailing in a fresh breeze with the spinnaker and blooper up, douse them quickly. In severe conditions run downwind so that the sails are blanketed, oversheet and lower them, blooper first, and get them belowdecks before coming beam to wind.

One experienced yachtsman suggests that if you are sailing downwind with the spinnaker up, round up and back the spinnaker. You will then be about two boat lengths from the person in the water. If you are sailing upwind, round up, back the jib, and heave-to alongside the victim. Start the engine for more control but make sure there are no lines overboard to foul the prop, and that the person in the water is not within the propeller's range. Leave the main up for stability.

If you lose visual contact with the person in the water you must carry out a precise navigational return to the victim such as a Williamson Turn (Figure 19). Assign piloting responsibilities to the most qualified crew member and follow instructions until the person is sighted.

When picking up the victim, rig a line amidships or use a transom ladder. Help the person aboard when the distance between deck and water is least. If the victim is helpless, rig a line with two loops through a snatch block at the end of the boom or the spinnaker halyard. A member of the crew can be lowered alongside with one loop around his own chest under his arms, while the other loop is placed around the victim. Both men can then be winched aboard. A bosun's chair can also be used in this method of recovery.

Reflecting on the safety procedures aboard *Tenacious* during the 1979 Fastnet, Robert Symonette commented: "In retrospect, it never occurred to me to think in terms of using life vests. . . . [but] after 2000 on the evening of the storm, no one in his right mind would have put his head out of the hatch without having a safety harness on. . . . *Tenacious* did not have a system of specific assignments of duties in the event of a man-overboard situation. Having been on *Figaro IV* when Dick Grossmiller went overboard in the Irish Sea in the Fastnet some years ago, I am very sensitive about this particular point. The 17 minutes Grossmiller spent overboard in the Irish Sea on my watch, with me at the helm, were perhaps the longest 17 minutes I have ever spent.

"I think it is very good practice to go through a man overboard drill on the way out to the start. Carleton Mitchell (owner of *Finisterre*), with whom I also raced, used to go so far as to assign specific responsibility for

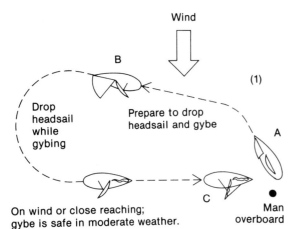

Wind

B

Drop
headsail
while
gybing

Prepare to drop
headsail and gybe

(1)

A

C

● Man
overboard

On wind or close reaching;
gybe is safe in moderate weather.

Figure 20: *The diagrams show
the optimum maneuvers for returning to a person overboard from all
points of sail and with running
sails up. (Reprinted by permission,
Sail magazine)*

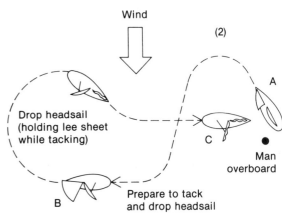

Wind

(2)

A

Drop headsail
(holding lee sheet
while tacking)

C

● Man
overboard

B

Prepare to tack
and drop headsail

On wind or close reaching;
gybe is not safe in fresh breeze.

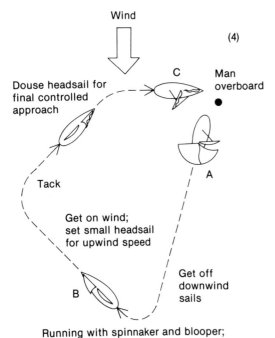

Wind

(4)

C   Man
overboard
●

Douse headsail for
final controlled
approach

A

Tack

Get on wind;
set small headsail
for upwind speed

Get off
downwind
sails

B

Running with spinnaker and blooper;
piloting very important

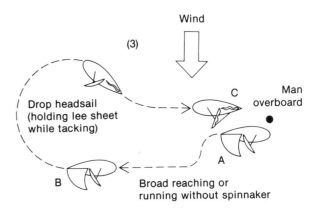

Wind

(3)

Drop headsail
(holding lee sheet
while tacking)

C   Man
overboard
●

A

B

Broad reaching or
running without spinnaker

148   Storm Sailing

Man Overboard Procedure

1. Throw the victim a life ring, horseshoe buoy, or Danbuoy marker.

2. One crewman watches the victim and, in fact, keeps pointing at him. He should stand at the highest vantage point possible.

3. The navigator starts a stopwatch immediately.

4. The helmsman records the compass course.

5. Get the boat under control and keep it there. Jibe as soon as possible. Mark the stopwatch at the jibe.

6. Sail back on a reciprocal course toward the victim. When the stopwatch time equals the period from the man overboard to the jibe, the victim should be in the vicinity.

7. Luff or heave-to.

8. Get a line around the victim and bring him aboard.

9. If the victim is injured, take a small jib with its head attached to the halyard and secure tack and clew to the stanchions on deck. With the head of the sail in the water, slide the victim into the sail and haul both on board.

the control of the ship in the event that he, himself, was washed overboard."

If You Are the One Overboard

The possibility of going overboard is not as remote as one thinks. Be prepared. Here are some rules that might aid in the recovery and keep you alive.

1. Keep contact with the boat, if possible. During the day, shout, wave your arms. Keep a whistle in your pocket. Blow it if you go over. The shrill sound of a whistle can be heard over wind and seas. At night, carry a waterproof pocket flashlight and use it. On a dark night you will be seen. If the boat comes near, splash the water, if conditions are not stormy.

2. Conserve your energy. If the water is relatively warm, float on your back; you will be more easily seen. If the water is cold and there is a danger of hypothermia, adopt the HELP position (see Appendix C).

VISUAL DISTRESS SIGNALS

Just as a yacht should not go to sea without its quota of PFDs, its horseshoe buoys, its radio communications, and its other safety equipment, it also should be prepared to call for help through the use of visual signals. The Coast Guard estimates that 45 percent of its rescue missions would be facilitated if visual distress signals were used.

In general, red, yellow, and orange contrast best against the sea. Fluorescent colors are easily distinguishable because they offer a brightness contrast as well as color contrast to the water. The Coast Guard suggests that the boat's underbody be painted a color that can be easily spotted—not the traditional blue or green. Also, a signal mirror in the sunlight can be seen to the horizon; it's an item that should be stowed aboard a life raft along with flares and other visual distress signals.

Here are some thoughts on the varieties and effectiveness of visual distress-signaling equipment available, as published in *Sail* magazine, and a listing of the signals themselves.

Visual distress signals should alert potential rescuers that your boat is in distress and/or enable them to find her position. Carry a variety because there is no one "best" distress signal. Consider effectiveness, recognizability, convenience, and cost in choosing which signals to carry. See Table 3.

• "Flashlights can be seen at night, but only if their batteries are new. Consider carrying a flashlight to be used solely in case of a distress situation.

• "Dye markers turn the water a bright fluorescent color when you pour them overboard. They are more

TABLE 3

Visual Distress Signal Effectiveness

Device	Detectability (in miles)
Daylight	
Red/orange balloon	½
Red two-star flare	½
Orange flight suit	½
Day/night flare	½
Red pen-gun flare	¾
Green dye marker[1]	2
White parachute	5
Orange smoke[2]	5
Signal mirror	5

[1]Greatly reduced in heavy seas
[2]Greatly reduced in high winds

Device	Detectability (in miles)
Darkness	
Electric floating lantern	1
Hand flashlight	3
Red Very signals	8
Aircraft marine markers	8
Day/night flare	8
Strobe lifejacket light	10
Red pen-gun flare	10
Red two-star flare	10

Estimates provided in the *National Search and Rescue Manual* (Reprinted by permission, *Sail* magazine)

visible from the air than from the surface. They dissipate very quickly in all but calm water.

• "Distress flags (orange squares with a black disc and square superimposed) should be waved frantically to be effective. Otherwise they might be misunderstood or ignored by passersby.

• "Signal mirrors are effective over wide ranges of weather and for considerable distances. Their main limitation is the need for sunlight or bright haze. A big advantage of mirrors is that wind doesn't disrupt them (as it does smoke and flares).

• "Strobe lights have excellent range (about 10 miles) and are excellent for position location. However, they are not very widely recognized as indications of distress.

• "Pyrotechnic signals include smoke and aerial flares. They are more sophisticated and more hazardous than simpler devices. Some, especially those shot from flare guns and 'pen-guns,' are legally considered as firearms in some states and must be registered as such. Never activate them in the presence of flammable vapors or fumes. Turn your face away when you set them off to avoid deflected gunpowder. Fire the projectile to leeward and at an upward angle to avoid having it return to the deck. Keep a hand-held flare at arm's length and angled away at about 45 degrees to minimize the drip of hot residue on your hand, raft, or boat.

"For all the problems they present, pyrotechnics are still the most universally recognized signal of distress at sea. They are also effective in many different conditions. If you combine them with a powerful signal for day (a mirror), night (a strobe), and fog (a horn), you have a versatile assortment that should be a big help in helping rescuers help you."

Signals indicating a vessel in distress requiring assistance include:

1. A gun or other explosive signal fired at intervals of about one minute.

2. A continuous sounding with any fog signaling apparatus.

3. Rockets or shells throwing red stars fired one at a time at short intervals.

4. A signal made by radiotelegraphy or by any other signaling method consisting of the Morse code SOS ($\cdots$ $--$ $\cdots$).

5. A signal sent by radiotelephone consisting of the spoken word MAYDAY.

6. The International Code Signal of distress indicated by code flags "NC."

7. A signal consisting of a square flag having above or below it a ball or anything resembling a ball.

8. Flames or smoke from a burning oil barrel.

9. A rocket parachute flare or a hand flare showing a red light.

10. A smoke signal giving off a volume of orange-colored smoke.

11. Slowly and repeatedly raising and lowering arms outstretched to each side.

12. An Ensign hoisted upside down.

13. An Ensign made fast, high in the rigging.

14. A piece of clothing attached to an oar or spar held up in the air.

15. A piece of orange material with a black square and a circle on it.

COMMUNICATIONS: Calling for Help

Offshore in the empty ocean, the only way of letting the world know about an emergency aboard your yacht is by use of radio (VHF or SSB), EPIRB, or Morse code. Not everyone knows how to go about it, however; this chapter offers basic information for skippers and crew in using the boat's radio equipment to summon aid. For further discussion, see Chapter 22 in Chapman's *Piloting, Seamanship & Small Boat Handling* (Hearst Marine Books).

All vessels are obliged to render assistance where possible to vessels in distress. Distress calls (Mayday) are made when a vessel or a person on board is in imminent and serious danger, and requires immediate assistance. Distress calls take priority over all other communications. If the situation doesn't warrant use of the distress call, but you have a very urgent message concerning the safety of a vessel or person, use the urgency call (PAN). For instance, if medical advice is required but life is not in danger, or if there is a possible *developing* emergency aboard your vessel, use the urgency call.

To summon help, call via VHF (Very High Frequency) Channel 16, SSB in the Medium Wave band (2182 kHz), or, near shore, via CB. A non-voice means is the EPIRB (Emergency Position Indicating Radio Beacon, as mentioned earlier). Do not use the international distress signal Mayday unless life or property is in danger. For a less serious emergency, if you are sailing in U.S. coastal waters, call the Coast Guard. It monitors VHF Channel 16, which has a range of about 20 miles from the coast, and 2182 kHz on SSB radio for calls beyond VHF range.

VHF is static free and can be homed in on by the Coast Guard. Channel 16 is the primary distress frequency and is never used for other traffic. The Coast Guard also uses Channel 22 as a talk channel.

The primary CB channel is Channel 9, which is monitored in some regions by the Coast Guard. CB, however, has a high degree of static, is usually full of chatter, and cannot be tracked by the Coast Guard's direction-finding equipment.

EPIRBs are monitored by satellites as well as by military and civilian aircraft and shore units. Signals have been picked up as far as 300 miles away. EPIRBs should be kept on board in readily accessible locations, and also stowed in the life raft.

Distress Call Procedures

Type up the distress call routine for your boat and tape it close to the radio, so that any member of the crew can find it and use it. Caution the crew not to shout into the microphone because shouting will distort the voice and make identification by the receiving vessel or Coast Guard much more difficult. Give the message even if there is no response, and keep giving it, because someone may hear you and relay the message to the Coast Guard or other authorities.

Via VHF, depress the mike switch and make the call according to the checklist on page 156. Note that your actual distress message should include the word "Mayday," followed by the name and call letters of your boat, position, nature of distress, and identification of the yacht in terms of color, sail number, etc. Afterwards, you can also transmit the nature of the aid required and any other information that will help the yacht. Here's how a Mayday distress call might sound:

"(Alarm signal, if available for 30 to 60 seconds.) Mayday, Mayday, Mayday. This is Yacht *Spindrift*, yacht *Spindrift*, yacht *Spindrift*, WZY 1234.

"Mayday, Yacht *Spindrift*, WYZ 1234. 133 degrees true, 12 miles from Montauk Point. Struck submerged object, taking on water fast, engine disabled. Estimate cannot stay afloat more than one hour. Six persons on board. *Spindrift* is a 42-foot sloop, white hull, green trim. Maintaining watch on Channel 16. This is Yacht *Spindrift*, WYZ 1234. Over."

Generally, if you reach the Coast Guard, it will ask for a long count so that it can fix its position-finding equipment on your transmitter. After that, it's a matter of time until the Coast Guard arrives by either boat or helicopter. Be precise in your message as to extent of damage, if any, medical emergency, position, and yacht description.

Equipment Considerations

The Ocean Racing Council recommends that yachts carry a marine radio transmitter and receiver with a minimum transmitter power of 25 watts. If the regular antenna is at the masthead, an alternate emergency antenna must be provided.

It is also recommended that yachts fitted with VHF transceivers install (for non-synthesized sets) Channel 72. This is an international ship-to-ship channel which, "by common use," would become an accepted yacht-to-yacht channel for all ocean racing yachts anywhere in the world. All yachts should also carry a radio receiver capable of receiving weather information.

After the 1979 Fastnet Race, it was discovered that many smaller yachts carried receivers with no transmitters. The ability to transmit would have helped in the rescue operations as would other navigational equipment (Loran C). Participants would then have been more exact about where they were located. It was felt that lives could have been saved if participants could have talked to other boats or rescue and medical personnel.

The successful use of EPIRBs is now well documented. The yacht *Ariel* is a typical example. In distress

TABLE 4

Emergency Broadcast Checklist

Radio operation

---

1. Turn on radio.
2. Select Channel 16.
3. Turn squelch up until static is heard.
4. Set volume.
5. Turn squelch down until static just disappears.
6. Key microphone to speak, release to listen.
7. Speak in a normal tone of voice, as on telephone.

Radio procedure

---

1. Key mike, repeat *Mayday* three times, state name and call letters of vessel.
2. Release mike and await reply.
3. With or without reply, repeat *Mayday* and proceed with following information:
4. Name of vessel (said three times);
5. Present position of vessel;
6. Nature of distress (fire, sinking, medical, etc);
7. Description of vessel—length, color, type (sloop, schooner);
8. Number of persons onboard;
9. If you are under way state course and speed, or state if you are anchored or drifting.

(Reprinted by permission, *Sail* magazine)

off Barnegat, New Jersey, she activated a Narco EPIRB. No fewer than 11 commercial air flights reported hearing the emergency transmitter within three hours, and the resulting multiple lines of position made it possible to locate the boat's life raft in a matter of minutes once the Coast Guard aircraft had gone up. Never activate an EPIRB for a short period and then shut it down to save the batteries. The searchers will not be able to home in on you.

RESCUE BY HELICOPTER

If your emergency is measured in minutes and the Coast Guard has dispatched a helicopter to remove a crewman with a severe medical problem, to remove the entire crew, or to drop a pump in advance of the arrival of a Coast Guard vessel, there are certain procedures that are the responsibility of the skipper. Following these will greatly aid the Coast Guard in making the transfer go as smoothly and as quickly as possible. Remember, even though you may have called for a helicopter, the Coast Guard will make the final decision about one, because there are times when weather obviates the use of a chopper.

Helicopter Rescue Checklist

This checklist covers most items that are of concern to rescue helo and vessel crews. Extraordinary conditions may require deviation from the norm, so be sure to *pay attention* to the helo crew during briefing, and be sure to let them know of any special circumstances on board your vessel.

Initial distress call:
Use VHF/FM Channel 16 or other emergency frequency.
Activate EPIRB for location and homing.
Give: boat name and radio call sign, your situation (indicating degree of emergency and any problems), your position,

continued

Helicopter Rescue Checklist *continued*

description of boat and any special markers, number of people on board.

Preparing the boat:

Lower, furl, and lash all sails.

Remove all unnecessary sheets, halyards, and lines.

Remove all gear from deck.

Have gear ready to remove (or cut) leeward lifelines and remove stanchions from bases.

Remove all gear from cockpit.

Remove all unused antennae from pulpits as well as fishing rods and man-overboard poles.

Place flares in a dry accessible place (near companionway).

Locate and check radio jury-rig antennae.

Rig cabintop marker flag or make reflective tape marker.

Rig boom to starboard and secure with vang or lashing.

Maneuvering the boat:

Head 30 to 45 degrees off the wind on port tack.

Keep sufficient way on to permit effective steering. Be prepared to handle boat in heavy winds.

Communications:

Do not change channels once communication is established.

Use proper radio procedure to avoid confusion.

Repeat instructions to guarantee understanding.

Find out how many people are aboard helicopter.

Ask for instructions to be repeated if you do not understand helo briefing.

Hoisting:

Tag patient, indicating medication given or other conditions that should be known by doctor (time tourniquet applied, for example).

Have crew in life jackets. Put life jacket on patient and strap in litter with hands inboard, clear of sides.

Determine crew hoisting order, injured first. Be sure flotation chest pad is in place on stretcher victim.

Allow stretcher or basket to contact metal part of boat firmly to discharge static electricity. Wear gloves to grab basket.

Do not secure trail line, cable, basket, or stretcher to boat.

Use trail line to steady stretcher or basket. Keep the line clear of the rigging, pulpits, and crew. Keep tension on the line.

continued

ABANDONING SHIP:

Life Rafts, Survival Tactics

At the first gale warning, double-lash the life raft on deck, preferably on a pair of strong chocks mounted on the cabin top. Secure it firmly (but still with quick release possible) so that heavy seas cannot wash it overboard. Lash it with canvas hold-downs or use a hydrostatic releasing device that will automatically deploy your raft at a pre-set depth of water, in case of a collision at sea or if you are run down.

Do not abandon your boat prematurely. Offshore sailor Arnie Gay says not to go "until you have to step *up* to do it." Keep bailing and pumping till the last possible moment. Often, derelict boats are found floating after being abandoned.

Drill the crew in the deployment of the life raft. Be sure to pull out a few feet of the painter and make it fast on a nearby cleat before you throw the raft cannister overboard.

If you are coastal cruising you should carry provisions adequate for one week aboard the life raft. If you are sailing offshore, provisions should be adequate for four weeks. Along with canned rations, provisions for four people for one week should include: two can openers (stored separately); eight (14 oz) cans of sweetened, condensed milk; two boxes (72 packages per box) of dextrose packed in three Ziploc bags; and one bottle of vitamins (28 high-potency with minerals, 28 B-complex).

The average person requires one pint of water per day. Canned water should be opened and checked during annual maintenance. If you plan to carry plastic containers on your life raft, fill the bottles only two-thirds to three-quarters of the way full—so they will float and be visible in the water. It is also a good idea to tie them together with a line.

If necessary, water collection can be done with a plastic sheet or space blanket by funneling water into a bailing bucket and then pouring it into other containers. A solar still converts sea water to fresh water by a natural evaporation-condensation process that produces about a quart of water a day in sunny weather, and about twenty ounces in cloudy weather.

A good survival kit is an essential piece of equipment on any life raft. The following is a good example of what should be included in a life-raft survival kit (reprinted by permission, *Sail* magazine):

1. Floating sheath knife
2. At least 1 solar still for every 2 people; 1 quart water per person
3. Fishing kit (variety of small and large hooks, varying weights line, sinkers, swivels, pliers, dried and canned bait)
4. 1 graduated plastic cup with screw-on lid (available in general merchandise stores)
5. 2 signaling mirrors
6. 1 waterproof signaling light with spare batteries and lamp bulbs packed in watertight plastic bag

7. Flares: 12 parachute, 6 hand, 2 orange smoke

8. 1 plastic bucket/bailers (plastic paint or ice cream buckets) with lanyards

9. 1 package of gallon-sized Ziploc plastic bags

10. 1 space blanket per person

11. Food

12. First-aid kit

13. 100 feet of light line (preferably type that floats and ties easily)

14. 2 sponges

15. Navigation equipment and charts

A first-aid kit is also a necessity for every life raft. Check with your doctor. Be sure to include any special medication that anyone in the crew might need in addition to what is outlined here (reprinted by permission, *Sail* magazine):

1. Anti-seasickness pills (minimum 6 per person)

2. Anti-diarrhea pills (minimum 6 per person)

3. 1 4-oz PABA lotion (sunburn prevention)

4. Stainless scissors with blunt ends (or scissors from patching kit)

5. Hexachlorophene-type lotion (for saltwater sores)

6. Adhesive tape that adheres in saltwater environment (in watertight package)

7. Gauze, waterproof bandages, and safety pins (watertight package)

8. Petroleum jelly

9. Eye lotion

10. Sunburn cream

11. Surgical needles and sutures (in watertight package)

12. One kind general antibiotic

13. One kind general pain reliever

RESCUES AT SEA: Aiding a Boat in Distress

It is every mariner's duty to come to the aid of a vessel in distress even if it only means standing by until a far more effective rescue team (i.e. Coast Guard) can take over. For some sailors, this is inbred; for junior racers at the Beachwood (N.J.) Yacht Club, it was mandatory that the closest sailboat stand by with a capsized boat until a rescue boat came to its aid. The first thing we checked was the safety of the crew of the capsized craft. It was something we took very seriously.

The noted skipper and author Capt. Felix Reisenberg is quoted as saying "the sea is selective, slow of recognition of effort and aptitude, but fast sinking the unfit." Equipment can break, a boat can go aground or hit a reef, crew members can be injured, but, if someone can get to the vessel in distress reasonably quickly there is no reason why the members of the crew cannot be taken off safely. The rescue boat's skipper must of course decide whether he is putting his own boat and crew in jeopardy. Over the past ten years, however, there have been a number of instances in ocean racing where prompt action by fellow skippers prevented loss of life.

In the 1981 SORC, racing on *Midnight Sun* we were neck and neck with *Bla Carat* 30 miles from the finish line when *Bla Carat* ahead and to leeward was suddenly dismasted. We bore off to stand by while her crew had picked the wreckage out of the water. Although we were losing time and distance in the race, we stood by until we were certain that the crew was safe. Then we continued on to the finish line and applied to the SORC Committee for an allowance equal to the time we had stood by. It was granted, in a practice that is now well established and actively encouraged.

In the 1974 SORC, the yacht *Wimoweh* miscalculated her position at night and ran afoul of a reef near Great Isaac on her way to Nassau. Another participant in the Miami-Nassau Race, the yacht *Osprey*, rescued the entire crew and went on to the finish. When the extra time that *Osprey* had spent in the rescue effort was subtracted from her elapsed time, she ended up as the Miami-Nassau winner. Although there was some controversy surrounding the awarding of extra time, which, incidentally did not include the extra crew weight on board, most yachtsmen heralded *Osprey's* effort.

There are times, however, when it is impossible to go to a rescue. During the height of the Fastnet storm, urgent SOS messages were being heard over the VHF from all directions. It was impossible to maneuver that night and also heed the calls of all of the boats asking for help. In that situation, it was deemed best to look after our own vessel, *Tenacious*, and count on the Royal Navy handling the distress calls.

When coming to the aid of a boat in distress, first establish communication by radio to determine the extent of the problem. Is there an injured crew member on board? How serious is the injury? What is the condition of the boat? Rapidly taking on water that the pumps can't handle? Or is the vessel aground? If she is aground, is it on a sand shoal or a reef? With appropriate wave action a reef can take the bottom out of a fiberglass boat in very short order.

If you have the slightest doubt whether you can successfully aid the boat in distress, call for additional help immediately—including the Coast Guard. Be sure to give an accurate position and the markings of your own boat, and state that you are on station in the vicinity of the craft in distress. Make sure, despite the urgency of the situation, that you keep a careful log of events from the time you receive the distress call until the time you depart.

Before you approach the vessel in distress, make sure your crew is ready for action with each member assigned to a specific task. Approach from leeward and straight into the wind, to minimize the effect of rolling. Each situation is different; wind and wave conditions may dictate alternate procedures. But, in general, try to get a line on board the vessel in distress, taking care to

check water depth so that your boat doesn't go aground too. If the seas are high, it will probably be impossible to bring the two boats together without damaging the rescuing boat. A better technique, one that has proved successful in a number of instances, is using a rubber dinghy to transfer crew. Rescue crew should not go into the water except in dire emergency.

Although it didn't seem so at the time, the rescue of the crew of the 40-foot Standfast sloop *Mary E* during the 1975 Miami-Nassau Race is a classic example of how teamwork and excellent seamanship can save lives, if not a boat. The *Mary E,* leading her class in a 40-knot gale that was whipping up 12-foot Gulf Stream waves, began to founder 14 miles west of Great Isaac light. First on the scene was the Carter 39 *Phoenix,* which, despite difficulties in finding the *Mary E,* managed to get to her, get a line on board, winch the two boats together, and take off three crew before the line parted and the two boats separated. Next to arrive was the sloop *J&B,* co-skippered by Mort Engel and sailmaker Jack Sutphen. It was Engel who suggested that the crew of the *Mary E* remove a submersible strobe from one of the personal harnesses, attach it to a halyard, and raise it to the top of the mast to mark the boat's position. Rescue took eight hours, until the *Mary E's* crew were all transferred to the rescue vessel by use of an Avon dinghy. Efforts to drop pumps from Coast Guard helicopters were unsuccessful, and it wasn't until a Coast Guard vessel reached the scene, guided by the strobe on the *Mary E's* mast, that *J&B* continued on to Nassau. She had been on station for eight hours.

In retrospect, three moves seem to stand out in the *Mary E* rescue. One crew member recalls that the Avon was the only viable way of transferring crew; the six-man life raft used for transferring gear was useless because the crew couldn't enter the hatches in the permanent canopy without first jumping into the water. Its canopy also made the life raft a victim of the wind. Significant too was the fact that the *Mary E* had lowered

"In retrospect the Avon was the only viable way of transferring the crew."

her sails and streamed a sea anchor, which held her in position. *J&B's* Jack Sutphen said later, "in the ten passes we made, the *Mary E* had not varied her position in the wind by five degrees." And the hoisted strobe very successfully guided both rescue vessels and the Coast Guard to the *Mary E,* when radar proved ineffective because of the number of racing vessels in the area.

CAPSIZING IN SMALL BOATS

Most often, you capsize in a dinghy because there is too much wind for the amount of sail being carried, because the boat is out of control, because skipper and crew are not paying attention, because there is an imbalance of weight, because you are caught in rapidly shifting winds (in both velocity and direction), or because you are trying to jibe in a strong wind with the centerboard up too far.

As a vital safety procedure in small-boat sailing, you should understand the forces at work when a boat capsizes. You should also know how to avoid those forces, and know what to do if somehow you cannot avoid them and do go over.

In the basic capsize, the boat is blown over to leeward with no sudden course change. A sudden increase in wind velocity makes the boat heel. Heeling reduces the "static" righting moment and boat speed is then reduced, which reduces the "kinetic" stability.

Heeling can also prevent the main from being eased enough to spill power if the boom hits the water. The crew weight on the weather rail drives the leeward gunwale into the water, which may allow water to come into the boat, aggravating control problems.

To avoid heeling, ease the sheets and retrim them. Do not feather the boat, as this reduces boat speed.

Broaching on a broad reach or run is another common reason for capsizing. The main impetus to broaching is heeling too much to leeward in the first place, and

the end result of course is a capsize to leeward. Broaching is precipitated by a sudden rounding up to weather as the result of overdoing the desire to head up slightly, or from the rudder stalling out. To prevent this, keep the rudder well within safety margins by limiting how much you heel.

The moment after a jibe is also a particularly inviting time for broaching. To prevent a broach, balance the boat so it is heeled to weather on the new jibe at the instant the boom flies over, and reverse the tiller through the middle of the jibe to cancel the turning moment (S jibe).

A "death roll to windward" is a sudden imbalance of forces that turns the boat sharply to leeward, and then either sudden crew weight movement or the force of the upper sail forces the boat over to windward. This is caused by the vang being too loose, which allows for too much twist and the boom being out too far while sailing very low or by the lee.

"Submarining" is pushing the bow into the wave ahead. Steering becomes impossible, the boat slows down and dramatically increases apparent wind. The cure for this is to move the weight aft and carefully keep the boat balanced sideways.

When sailing upwind, hitting a big header may cause the jib to back and you to capsize. The only cure for this is anticipation.

If you luff too much in heavy air, forward way is lost. Open bailers fill the boat with water, which destroys control and can cause you to capsize. Again, anticipation is the cure.

To counteract an imminent capsize to windward, lean into the boat, trim the main, and head the boat into the wind by pushing the tiller toward the sail. To leeward, ease the sails out so they begin to luff while heading the boat up into the wind, and hike out to keep the boat flat. Once the boat is heeling too far over, the rudder becomes ineffective.

Pick a safe course to sail. Straight downwind is the most likely to cause a capsize because of the chance of

In a dinghy capsize, stay with your boat until someone comes to your aid.
Carol Singer

an accidental jibe. And many capsizes are caused by too much boom vang. In heavy air ease the vang out to let the wind spill out the top of the mainsail.

After the Capsize

After you capsize (in a dinghy), all members of the crew should stay with the boat even if you are unable to right it. The rescue boat should always approach the capsized boat from the leeward side. If the sailors seem cold, get them out of the water immediately.

If the boat can be righted, have one of the sailors free the sheets and pull the boat head-to-wind by holding on to the bow line until the boat swings around. If the mast starts to sink put a life jacket under the tip of the mast to help keep it floating and to keep the boat from turning turtle. Use the centerboard as a lever and stand on it to right the boat. As the boat comes up, grab the side and continue to pull until the boat is upright. Rest, then pull yourself (the skipper) into the middle of the boat.

If the boat has turned turtle, try to right it by pulling on one jib sheet and the centerboard. If possible, unclip the sail at the clew. If the mast is wedged in mud, another boat should anchor directly upwind and throw a line to you. The wind and waves will pivot the boat into the wind and pull the mast out of the mud so you can right it.

From the rescue boat, pump the water out of the righted boat. When it is adequately pumped, board the boat from the stern and finish bailing. Check the boat to see that all equipment is there and undamaged.

If the boat is swamped, sit down and bail. Keep one person in the water to steady the boat. If a tow boat is available, lower the sails and secure all equipment to keep it from floating away. Attach a line from the tow boat to the foredeck cleat or around the base of the mast of the swamped boat. Have your boat towed into the wind at a slow speed. Keep the centerboard up, and keep your life jacket on, because a water-filled boat is very unstable.

In the self-rescuing one-design classes a procedure for requesting or refusing help when capsized has evolved. A clenched fist signifies "request help" and an open palm toward the rescue craft signifies "keep away." In severe conditions, however, the judgment of the rescue craft commander as to whether or not to intercede must overrule the wishes of the skipper, especially if the self-rescue efforts do not appear to be successful and other boats are in need of assistance.

ANCHORS AND ANCHORING

When you are caught near land at the onset of a storm, the last resort may be to anchor although it is generally far better to head out to sea and ride out the weather. Here are some notes on anchors and anchoring in heavy weather.

The two primary types of anchors are lightweight "burying" anchors (CQR and Danforth), and kedges, or "hooking" anchors, like the Herreshoff or Yachtsman types. Different kinds of anchors are best suited for different bottoms and different conditions, so the well-equipped cruising yacht may carry three anchors—a plow (CQR), a Danforth, and a kedge of some sort.

An anchor of ample weight is essential. Rule of thumb dictates that burying-type anchors weigh one pound for each foot of overall boat length while kedge-type anchors weigh two pounds per foot.

The holding power of an anchor can be improved by sliding a weight part-way down the anchor rode. Holding power also is increased (see diagram) by attaching at least six feet of chain to the anchor. The chain helps keep the anchor securely down on the seabed; rope, which is light, tends to lift the anchor stock as the boat moves at her anchorage, and in high winds the anchor

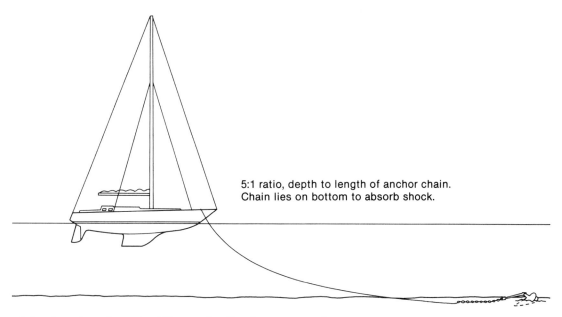

5:1 ratio, depth to length of anchor chain.
Chain lies on bottom to absorb shock.

might then lose its grip. The main disadvantages of rope-only anchor line is the problem of chafe; a rope will get chewed through in a matter of hours if the vessel is anchored in a rock or coral area. When anchoring, be sure to allow at least a five-to-one ratio of rode to depth; seven to one is even better. In heavy winds and seas, a longer anchor line is a necessity.

When storms threaten, have all anchors and warps on deck. Remember, a combination of windage, sheering loads, and jerking strains may overpower the ground tackle. Reduce windage by taking down awnings, flags, poles, antennas, radar reflectors, sails, and loose gear. Gusts and squalls above the level of the storm can impose severe side-to-side sheering loads. Jerking strains can come from unusual swells. A boat jerking hard against her chain in violent gusts may damage the anchor windlass, the samson post, the bow roller, or the chain stopper, or even break the cable. Ease this situation by taking the strain off the chain with a nylon line (with the chain of course still hooked up). A line or lines to land may also be an answer, depending on the conditions.

Figure 21: *A length of chain helps keep the anchor down and guards against surge that may cause dragging. Always anchor with enough rode to provide a low angle (about 5 to 7:1) depending upon conditions. This will also guard against dragging.*

Be especially careful of chafe on nylon anchor line. Use a heavy rubber radiator hose or plastic tubing two or three feet long, whose inside diameter is a tight fit for the nylon. Keep the hose in place with pieces of small line tied around the nylon rope above and below the chafing gear, or with metal hose clamps. Inspect this rig every several hours during a storm. It may need to be moved an inch or two to prevent chafing through.

During a storm, keep an anchor watch around the clock. One person should be awake and dressed, taking bearings to get the yacht's position and capable of getting the vessel underway at once if necessary. This is especially important if there is a chance other vessels may drag down on you, if the wind is strong and changeable, or if the holding ground is bad. If you begin to drag, use the engine to help hold your position or move off a lee shore.

Use your best anchor and longest line. Secure the line to the mast rather than to any deck fitting, and, to prevent chafing, consider using snatch blocks as fairleads rather than regular chocks. Use chafing gear as needed.

TOWING

There are three kinds of tows. Your disabled vessel may require one of them or a combination of all three. They are: (1) A short tow up a channel or off the mud; (2) Maneuvering a powerless boat to a berth; and (3) A long tow across open water. Each has different requirements in making the towed vessel fast to your boat. A short tow requires taking only a couple of turns of the tow line around a cleat or winch; hold the tail in your hand so it will not jam and so that it can be cast off quickly if necessary. Do not hold the rope too close to the bitter end in case it slips. A towing hitch is helpful but a single towing point may make the tow boat difficult to maneuver.

On a long tow, pass the tow rope around the mast or coachroof to distribute the strains. Also, distribute the load over a number of strong points rather than making the tow line fast to a single cleat or winch. For example, take one turn around a stern cleat with the tow line, then around a bow cleat and then another stern cleat, and secure the tow line back on itself aft of the transom with a rolling hitch, or secure it with a bridle aft of the transom. Anticipate problems of chafe. Protect around the fairleads and cleats with chafing gear and adjust the line periodically to move the strain to different parts.

For a long tow at sea, waves are the biggest problem because they impose added strains and violent jerks. To reduce this movement get some elasticity in the line. Use a nylon line that is as long as possible; in waves, the length of the tow line should be at least equal to the distance between crests. If you are towing in a harbor or canal and you have to keep the line short, attach a heavy weight in the middle of the line to create a curve (a chain is a good weight), and adjust the line's length so that the boats rise and fall on the waves at the same time. If necessary, the towed vessel may stream a drogue to stop her from overtaking the towing craft.

If you are the boat being towed, lead the tow line through a chock or fairlead as close to the stem as possible or use a bridle to lead the line over the stem. It is best to tie the tow rope to a samson post or the mast, if it is stepped through to the keel, or make it fast around the cabin top. Try to spread the load out over a number of strong points. You should be able to release the tow rope quickly.

Rig an anchor, watch for chafe in the tow line, and trim your boat down in the stern to keep the bow from digging in and sheering off. Steer for the center of the tow boat's transom, except of course when you both are turning. Then steer momentarily for her wake on the opposite side from the one to which she is turning—which will keep the tow line tight and the strain constant.

To maneuver a boat into its berth, first secure it alongside the tow boat with bow, stern, and spring lines that can be cast off quickly. Do this in protected water, use lots of fenders, and lash alongside solidly to form a sort of catamaran. But be sure not to have the masts abeam of each other as the spreaders may become entangled.

Remember that you will turn more rapidly toward the powerless vessel than away from it. When you apply reverse, the momentum of the towed boat will turn both bows in the direction of the boat applying the power. Two boats will take longer to stop than one. Someone should steer each hull. Increase power when approaching a wake to put strain on the lines and dampen the motion of the two boats. Put the tow boat aft on the quarter of the towed boat if the towed boat is a lot bigger. This will allow for maximum control.

Communicate between the tow boat and the towed boat. Agree upon signals before towing and use radio contact if possible. If you are towing in fog the tow boat should sound one long blast followed by two short (Morse code D for "I am maneuvering with difficulty"). The towed boat acknowledges this message with one long and three short blasts. This sequence should be repeated every two minutes.

To head off a difficult situation, use the danger signal (four short blasts or more) when approaching a congested channel or inlet while you are towing. And for added safety someone on the tow boat should always be watching the boat astern.

Rules of the Road for Towing

Under International Rules of the Road, a yacht has no special privileges or special right of way when towing *except* in a strong following current, when she may be considered a vessel "restricted in her ability to maneuver," and need only yield to vessels not under command, such as dredges, etc.

"It is best to tie a tow rope to the mast if it is stepped on the keel. . . ."

174   Storm Sailing

By day, when restricted in ability to maneuver, fly two red balls with a white diamond between them, displayed in a vertical line. By night, use three vertical lights—red-white-red.

When towing under normal conditions by day—fly a black diamond shape. By night—display normal sidelights, a white masthead light, and a stern light. In addition, display a second white masthead light vertically above the normal one and a second stern light (yellow) above the normal one. If the length of your tow line is more than 200 meters, a third white masthead light should be carried over the other two. Spacing between vertical lights should be at least 1 meter.

The boat being towed should display normal sidelights and a sternlight. If the tow line is over 200 meters, a diamond shape should be added.

Towing and the Law

Salvage law and precedent say that the tower is entitled to a "fair reward for his services." However, no salvage claim can be made unless your boat is actually in danger, and unless you accept the tow. Make any financial arrangements with the tow boat *before* accepting service. Control as much of the operation as you can. Do not take a member of the towing vessel's crew on board unless necessary, to avoid heavier fees and/or claims for salvage.

Conclusion — Some Notes on Storm Sailing

While researching this book and digging into my own experience with heavy weather, several conclusions become inescapable:

The boat must be rigged and prepared thoroughly for storm sailing if it is going to venture offshore either to race or to cruise.

The boat with the best chance of survival, provided it is prepared, is the one with the most experienced crew.

Ted Turner, with whom I sailed on *Courageous* and *Tenacious,* has confirmed this in discussions we have had over the years. . . .

On the question of preparation and equipment:

"Fortunately, I always have had strong boats. I have not allowed myself to get caught up in the craze for light boats and equipment. When the wind starts to really come on, it's better to be prepared than to have to go right to the edge. When you get down to storm canvas, not much can go wrong. You are not likely to lose your rig if you have a strong stick in the boat."

And, on the question of crew, Turner sums it up this way:

"The roughest conditions I've encountered were during the winter cruises when I first started ocean racing and we were shorthanded. My crews were not experienced and we got into trouble more than once. But over the last ten years (prior to his retirement from ocean racing) we've always had a large and competent crew and we've always taken all of the precautions."

It was this attitude, even though Turner in 35 years at sea by his own admission had never experienced winds of more than 80 knots, that had allowed *Tenacious* to survive and win in the 1979 Fastnet.

There *is* something to be said for being at sea in heavy weather in a strong, well-prepared, well-manned vessel. The famed marine artist John Mecray has described such a passage aboard the schooner yacht *America* en route to Bermuda:

"Though perceptibly less cold, the winds had built to gale force and the seas had increased to about 20 feet, but they were long swells and *America's* great hull seemed to skim along in total harmony with her surroundings . . . as we measured an occasional gust at 65 knots.

"It developed into an artist's dream come true. The sun would break through patches in the low running clouds to spotlight the drama. The sea, where it wasn't a creamy foam, was black. As a swell would peak above us, its crest would glow an eerie green and blow away in a white mist, illuminated as if by some unworldly force.

"*America* never faltered, indeed she seemed very much at home. Great rollers approached us from astern as if to swallow the schooner whole, but she rose and soared along on her course at an average 12 knots.

"Then all too soon the cloud cover increased and the play of light diminished, leaving us in an undulating world of grey. It was a strange feeling indeed to feel let down as the tempest subsided. It was as if we had just been on the verge of witnessing a revelation of some great cosmic mystery, but as in a dream, awoke too soon."

And that, to me, is the essence of storm sailing.

List
of
Illustrations

Charisma *(previous page) shows her underbody as she makes her way closehauled in 35-knot winds during the 1976 SORC. The maxi-yacht* Condor *(above) takes 50-knot winds in stride during the 1979 Cowes Week with her large crew up to weather. Braving storm seas, a Whitbread Round-the-World racer (right) has a reefed main but should have it furled. Comfortably balanced,* Windward Passage *(far right) makes spectacular progress racing in heavy Pacific seas.*

Alastair Black   *Alastair Black*
Geoff Stagg   *Phil Uhl*

Unknowing preparation for the Fastnet storm occurs during the 1979 Cowes Week as the fleet begins a race in the Solent in 30-knot winds that built to 50 by the time the race ended (previous page).

Gary Jobson

Kialoa's crew (right) is in position on the windward rail, during the 1981 SORC, as Apollo (below) charges forward under reduced sail in the 1982 Clipper Cup. Tenacious *(far right) is impeccably trimmed for heavy weather during the 1981 SORC, as aboard* Midnight Sun *(below right) big sea sailing has its own beauty.*

Christopher Cunningham   Phil Uhl
Christopher Cunningham   Gary Jobson

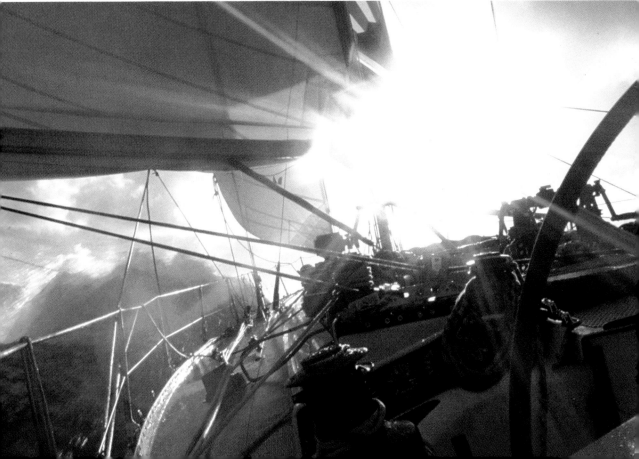

The result of wind opposing current can be seen in the 20-foot seas built up in the Gulf Stream (right) during the 1981 St. Petersburg-Ft. Lauderdale Race. The heavy seas resulted in Bla Carat's dismasting (below) 35 miles from the finish line. Standing by was the Holland 51, Midnight Sun, taking a beating (above). Even maxi-yachts are not immune from rigging failure. Condor (right) returns to home base (far right) after dismasting in the 1981 Maxi Worlds off Sardinia.

Gary Jobson

In the remarkable broach sequence on these pages photographer *Phil Uhl* caught **Secret Love** losing it during a race off Hawaii. Apparently the mistake came when, on a jibe (above), the crew let the spinnaker get around the headstay. Quick easing of the spinnaker sheet might have saved the situation, but came too late to prevent dunking (right).

Phil Uhl

The schooner yacht America *(left) takes 40-knot winds and big seas in stride off Guadeloupe. The Whitbread racer* Ceramco New Zealand *wings a jib out to windward on her spinnaker pole, as she keeps going despite gale conditions in the Southern Ocean.*

Alastair Black   *Geoff Stagg*

Some disasters in the making during heavy weather: Two Congressional Cup racers collide during the 1982 series after one of the Catalina 38s broaches (upper left). Zamazaan *takes a knockdown in San Francisco Bay (left). In a tussle between the maxi-yachts* Xargo *and* Kialoa, Kialoa's *crew eases off the spinnaker to bring her up. Even a light keel boat can deal with heavy breezes and good seas as this J-24 (following page). With a flattening reef in the main and vang tension, the crew is ready to collapse the spinnaker to keep the boat on its feet.*

Phil Uhl   Phil Uhl   Carol Singer

1.0 Purpose and Use

1.1 It is the purpose of these special regulations to establish uniform minimum equipment and accommodations standards for yachts racing under the International Offshore Rule and thereby to aid in promoting uniform offshore racing throughout the world.

1.2 These regulations do not replace, but rather supplement, the requirements of governmental authority, the Racing Rules and the International Offshore Rule. The attention of owners is called to restrictions in the rules on the location and movement of equipment.

1.3 The Offshore Racing Council strongly recommends the use of these special regulations by all organizations sponsoring races under the International Offshore Rule. Race Committees may select the category deemed most suitable for the type of race to be sailed. They are urged to depart from the regulations or modify or make exceptions hereto only when the most compelling circumstances so dictate.

APPENDIX A

ORC Standards for Equipment and Accommodations

2.0   Owner's Responsibility

2.1   The safety of a yacht and her crew is the sole and inescapable responsibility of the owner, or owner's representative who must do his best to ensure that the yacht is fully found, thoroughly seaworthy and manned by an experienced crew who are physically fit to face bad weather. He must be satisfied as to the soundness of hull, spars, rigging, sails and all gear. He must ensure that all safety equipment is properly maintained and stowed and that the crew know where it is kept and how it is to be used.

2.2   Neither the establishment of these special regulations, their use by sponsoring organizations, nor the inspection of a yacht under these regulations in any way limits or reduces the complete and unlimited responsibility of the owner or owner's representative.

2.3   It is the sole and exclusive responsibility of each yacht to decide whether or not to start or continue to race.

3.0   Inspection

3.1   A yacht may be inspected at any time. If she does not comply with these special regulations her entry may be rejected, or she will be liable to disqualification or such other penalty as may be prescribed by the national authority or the sponsoring organization.

4.0   Categories of Offshore Events

4.1   The International Offshore Rule is used to rate a wide variety of types and sizes of yachts in many types of races, ranging from long-distance ocean races sailed under adverse conditions to short-course day races sailed in protected waters. To provide for the differences in the standards of safety and accommodation required for such varying circumstances, four categories of races are established, as follows:

4.2   *Category 1 race.* Races of long distance and well offshore, where yachts must be completely self-sufficient for extended periods of time, capable of withstanding heavy storm and prepared to meet serious emergencies without the expectation of outside assistance.

4.3   *Category 2 race.* Races of extended duration along or not far removed from shorelines or in large unprotected bays or lakes, where a high degree of self-sufficiency is required of the yachts but with the reasonable probability that outside assistance could be called upon for aid in the event of serious emergencies.

4.4   *Category 3 race.* Races across open water, most of which is relatively protected or close to shorelines, including races for small yachts.

4.5   *Category 4 race.* Short races, close to shore in relatively warm or protected waters.

In the following lists:
(a)   The star indicates that the item applies to the category in that column.
(b)   For yachts not racing under the I.O.R., alternatives to the I.O.R. terms are indicated in brackets.

5.0   Basic Standards

5.1   All required equipment shall:
Function properly
Be readily accessible
Be of a type, size and capacity
suitable and adequate for the
intended use and size of the yacht

5.2   *Yachts shall be self-righting. They shall be strongly built, watertight and, particularly with regard to hulls, have decks and cabin trunks capable of withstanding solid water and knockdowns. They must be properly rigged and ballasted, be fully seaworthy and must meet the standards set forth herein.*

"Properly rigged" means (inter alia) that shrouds shall never be disconnected.

5.3   *Inboard engine installation shall be such that the engine, when running, can be securely covered, and that the exhaust and fuel supply systems are securely installed and adequately protected from the effects of heavy weather. When an electric starter is the only provision for starting the engine, a separate battery shall be carried, the primary purpose of which is to start the engine.*

5.4   *Yacht equipment and fittings shall be securely fastened so as to remain in position should the yacht be capsized 180°.*

5.5   *Yacht equipment and fittings shall be securely fastened.*

6.0   Structural Features

6.1   *The hull, including deck, coach roof and all other parts, shall* form an integral, essentially watertight, unit and any openings in it shall be capable of being immediately secured to maintain this integrity (see 5.1). For example, running rigging or control lines shall not compromise this watertight unit. Centerboard and daggerboard trunks shall not open into the interior of the hull.

6.12   *Hatches.* No hatches forward of the BMAX (maximum beam) station shall open inwards excepting ports having an area of less than 110 sq. in. (710cm²). Hatches shall be so arranged as to be above the water when the hull is heeled 90°. All hatches shall be permanently fitted so that they can be closed immediately and will remain firmly shut in a 180° capsize. The main companionway hatch shall be fitted with a strong securing arrangement which shall be operable from above and below.

6.13   *Companionways.* All blocking arrangements (washboards, hatch-boards etc.) shall be capable of being secured in position with the hatch open or shut and shall be secured to the yacht by lanyard or other mechanical means to prevent their being lost overboard.

6.14   *Cockpit companionways*, if extended below main deck level, must be capable of being blocked off to the level of the main deck at the sheer line abreast the opening. When such blocking arrangements are in place this companionway (or hatch) shall continue to give access to the interior of the hull.

6.21   *Cockpits* shall be structurally strong, self draining and permanently incorporated as an integral part of the hull. They must be essentially watertight, that is, all openings to the hull below the main deck level must be capable of being strongly and rigidly secured. Any bow, lateral, central or stern well will be considered as a cockpit for the purposes of 6.21, 6.22, 6.23 and 6.31.

6.22   *Cockpits opening aft to the sea.* The lower edge of the companionway shall not be below main deck level as measured above. The openings shall not be less than 50% of max. cockpit depth multiplied by max. cockpit width. The requirements in 6.31 that cockpits must drain at all angles of heel, applies.

6.23   *Cockpit volume.*

6.23.1   The maximum volume of all cockpits below lowest coamings shall not exceed 6% L times B times FA (6% loaded water line times maximum beam times freeboard abreast the cockpit). The cockpit sole must be at least 2% L above LWL (2% length overall above loaded water line).

6.23.2   The maximum volume of all cockpits below lowest coamings shall not exceed 9% L times B times FA (9% loaded water line times maximum beam times freeboard abreast the cockpit). The cockpit sole must at least 2% L above LWL (2% length overall above loaded water line).

6.31   *Cockpit drains.*

6.31.1   *For yachts 21 feet R (28 feet/8.53m length overall) and over.* Cockpit drains adequate to drain cockpits quickly but with a combined area (after allowance for screens, if attached) of not less than the equivalent of four ¾ in. (2 cm) diameter drains. Yachts built before 1-1-72 must have drains with a combined area (after allowance for screens, if attached) of not less than the equivalent of two 1 in. (2.5 cm) drains. Cockpits shall drain at all angles of heel.

Yachts built before 1-1-77 may conform to 6.31.2 for races in Categories 3 and 4.

6.31.2   *For yachts under 21 feet R (28 feet/8.52m length overall).* Cockpit drains adequate to drain cockpits quickly but not less in combined area (after allowance for screens, if attached) than the equivalent of two 1 in. (2.5 cm) diameter drains. Cockpits shall drain at all angles of heel.

6.4   *Storm covering* for all windows more than two square feet in area.

6.51   *Sea cocks or valves* on all through-hull openings below LWL, except integral deck scuppers, shaft log, speed indicators, depth finders and the like; however, a means of closing such openings, when necessary to do so, shall be provided.

Does not apply in Category 4 races to yachts built before 1-1-76.

6.52   Soft wood plugs, tapered and of various sizes.

6.53   *Ballast and heavy equipment.*

Inside ballast in a yacht shall be securely fastened in position. All other heavy internal fittings (such as batteries, stoves, gas bottles, tanks, engines, out-board motors, etc.) and anchors and chains (see 8.31 and 8.32) shall be securely fastened against a capsize.

6.54   *Sheet winches* shall be mounted in such a way

that no operator is required to be substantially below deck.

6.6 Life-lines, Stanchions and Pulpits

6.61 *For all yachts.*

6.61.1 *Life-line terminals.* A taut lanyard of synthetic rope may be used to secure life-lines, provided that when in position its length does not exceed 4 ins. (10cm).

6.61.2 *Stanchions shall* not be angled from the point of their attachment to the hull at more than ten degrees from vertical throughout their length.

6.61.3 *Overlapping pulpits.* Life-lines need not be affixed to the bow pulpit if they terminate at, or pass through, adequately braced stanchions 2 ft. (60cm) (18 ins. (45cm) for yachts under 21 feet R (28 feet/8.53m length overall) above the working deck, set inside and overlapping the bow pulpit, provided that the gap between the upper life-line and the bow pulpit does not exceed 6 ins. (15cm).

6.61.4 *Pulpit and stanchion fixing.* Pulpits and stanchions shall be through-bolted or welded, and the bases thereof shall not be further inboard from the edge of the working deck than 5% of B max. (maximum beam) or 6 ins. (15cm), whichever is greater. Stanchion bases shall not be situated outboard of the working deck.

6.62 *For yachts of 21 feet R (28 feet/8.53m length overall) and over.*

6.62.1 *Taut double life-lines,* with upper life-line of wire at a height of not less than 2 ft. (60cm) above the working deck, to be permanently supported at intervals of not more than 7 ft. (2.15m). When the cockpit opens aft to the sea, additional life-lines must be fitted so that no opening is greater in height than 22 ins. (56cm).

6.62.2 *Pulpits.* Fixed bow pulpit (forward of headstay) and stern pulpit (unless life-lines are arranged as to adequately substitute for a stern pulpit). Lower life-lines need not extend through the bow pulpit. Upper rails of pulpits shall be at not less height above the working deck than upper life-lines. Upper rails in bow pulpits shall be securely closed while racing.

Any life-line attachment point will be considered as a stanchion in so far as its base shall not be situated outboard of the working deck.

6.63 *For yachts under 21 feet R (28 feet/8.53m length overall).*

6.63.1 *Taut single wire life-line,* at a height of not less than 18 ins. (45cm) above the working deck, to be permanently supported at intervals of not more than 7 ft. (2.15m). If the life-line is at any point more than 22 ins. (56cm) above the rail cap, a second intermediate life-line must be fitted. If the cockpit opens aft to the sea additional life-lines must be fitted so that no opening is greater in height than 22 ins. (56cm).

6.63.2 *Pulpits.* Fixed bow pulpit and stern pulpit (unless life-lines are arranged as to adequately substitute for a stern pulpit). Lower life-lines need not extend through the bow pulpit. Upper rails of pulpits must be at no less height above the working deck than upper life-lines. Upper rails in bow pulpits shall be securely closed while racing. The bow pulpit may be fitted abaft the forestay with its bases secured at any points on deck, but a point on its upper rail must be within 16 ins. (40cm) of the forestay on which the foremost headsail is hanked.

Any life-line attachment point will be considered as a stanchion so far as its base shall not be situated outboard of the working deck.

6.64 *Toe rails.* A toe-rail of not less than 1 in. (2.5cm) shall be permanently fitted around the deck forward of the mast, except in way of fittings. Location to be not further inboard from the edge of the working deck than one third of the local beam.

A third life-line (or second for yachts under 21 ft. R (28 feet/8.53m length overall) at a height of not less than 1 in. (2.5cm) or more than 2 ins. (5cm) above the working deck will be accepted in place of a toe-rail.

In yachts built before 1 January 1981 a toe-rail of ¾ in. (2cm) will be accepted.

7.0   Accommodations

7.11   *Toilet,* securely installed.

7.12   *Toilet,* securely installed, or fitted bucket.

7.2   *Bunks,* securely installed.

7.31   *Cooking stove,* securely installed against a capsize with safe accessible fuel shutoff control capable of being safely operated in a seaway.

7.32   Cooking stove, capable of being safely operated in a seaway.

7.41   *Galley facilities,* including sink.

7.42   Galley facilities.

7.51   *Water tanks,* securely installed and capable of dividing the water supply into at least two separate containers.

7.52   At least one securely installed water tank.

7.53   At least 2 gallons (9 litres) of water for emergency use carried in one or more separate containers.

7.54   Suitable containers for water.

8.0   General Equipment

8.1   *Fire extinguishers,* at least two, readily accessible in suitable and different parts of the boat.

8.21.1   *Bilge pumps,* at least two manually operated, securely fitted to the yacht's structure, one operable above, the other below deck. Each pump shall be operable with all cockpit seats, hatches and companionways shut.

8.21.2 Each bilge pump shall be provided with permanently fitted discharge pipe(s) of sufficient capacity to accommodate simultaneously both pumps.

8.21.3 No bilge pumps may discharge into a cockpit unless that cockpit opens aft to the sea. Bilge pumps shall not be connected to cockpit drains.

8.21.4 Unless permanently fitted, each bilge pump handle shall be provided with a lanyard or catch or similar device to prevent accidental loss.

8.22 One manual bilge pump operable with all cockpit seats, hatches and companionways closed.

8.23 One manual bilge pump.

8.24 Two buckets of stout construction each with at least 2 galls. (9 litres) capacity. Each bucket to have a lanyard.

8.31 *Anchors.* Two with cables except yachts rating under 21 feet R (28 feet/8.53m length overall) which shall carry at least one anchor and cable.
Anchors and any chain shall be securely fastened in the position recorded on the Rating Certificate when not in use.

8.32 One anchor and cable.
Anchor(s) and any chain shall be securely fastened in the position recorded on the Rating Certificate when not in use.

8.41 *Flashlights,* one of which is suitable for signalling, water resistant, with spare batteries and bulbs.

8.42 At least one flashlight, water resistant, with spare batteries and bulb.

8.5 *First aid kit* and manual.

8.6 *Foghorn.*

8.7 *Radar reflector.* If a radar reflector is octahedral it must have a minimum diagonal measurement of 18 ins. (46 cm), or if not octahedral must have a documented 'equivalent echoing area' of not less than 10m².

8.8   *Set of international code flags* and international code book.

8.9   *Shutoff valves* on all fuel tanks.

9.0   Navigation Equipment

9.1   *Compass,* marine type, properly installed and adjusted.

9.2   *Spare compass.*

9.3   *Charts, light list and piloting equipment.*

9.4   *Sextant, tables and accurate time piece.*

9.5   *Radio direction finder.*

9.6   *Lead line or echo sounder.*

9.7   *Speedometer or distance measuring instrument.*

9.8   *Navigation lights,* to be shown as required by the International Regulations for Preventing Collision at Sea, mounted so that they will not be masked by sails or the heeling of the yacht.
     Yachts under 7m LOA shall comply with the regulations for those between 12m and 7m LOA (i.e. they shall exhibit sidelights and a sternlight).

10.0   Emergency Equipment

10.1   *Emergency navigation lights* and power source.

10.21   *The following specifications for mandatory sails give maximum areas; smaller areas may well suit some yachts.*

10.21.1 *One storm trysail* not larger than 0.175 P × E in area. It shall be sheeted independently of the boom and shall have neither a headboard nor battens and be of suitable strength for the purpose. The yacht's sail number and letter(s) shall be placed on both sides of the trysail in as large a size as is practicable.

10.21.2 *One storm jib* of not more than 0.05 IG^2 (5% height of the foretriangle squared) in area, the luff of which does not exceed 0.65 IG (65% height of the foretriangle), and of suitable strength for the purpose.

10.21.3 *One heavy-weather jib* of suitable strength for the purpose with area not greater than 0.135 IG^2 (13.5% height of the foretriangle squared) and which does not contain reef points.

10.22   One heavy-weather jib as in 10.21.3 (or heavy-weather sail in a boat with no forestay) and either—

    (a)   a storm trysail as in 10.21.1 or

    (b)   mainsail reefing equipment capable of reducing the effective luff to 60% P or less.

10.23   Any storm or heavy-weather jib if designed for a seastay or luff-groove device shall have an alternative method of attachment to the stay or a wire luff.

10.24   No mast shall have less than two halyards each capable of hoisting a sail.

10.3   *Emergency steering equipment*

10.31   An emergency tiller capable of being fitted to the rudder stock.

10.32   Crews must be aware of alternative methods of steering the yacht in any sea condition in the event of rudder failure. An inspector may require that this method be demonstrated.

10.4   *Tools and spare parts*, including adequate means to disconnect or sever the standing rigging from the hull in the case of need.

10.5   *Yacht's name* on miscellaneous buoyant equipment, such as life jackets, oars, cushions, etc. Portable sail number.

10.61   *Marine radio transmitter and receiver.* If the regular antenna depends upon the mast, an emergency antenna must be provided.

Yachts fitted with VHF transceivers are recommended to install VHF Channel 72 (156.625 MHz Simplex). This is an international ship-ship channel, which, by "common use," could become an accepted yacht-yacht channel for all ocean racing yachts anywhere in the world.

10.62 *Radio receiver* capable of receiving weather bulletins.

11.0 Safety Equipment

11.1 *Life jackets,* one for each crew member.

11.2 *Whistles* attached to life jackets.

11.3 *Safety belt* (harness type) one for each crew member.

Each yacht may be required to demonstrate that two thirds of the crew can be adequately attached to strong points on the yacht.

11.41 *Life raft(s)* capable of carrying the entire crew and meeting the following requirements:

A.   Must be carried on the working deck or in a special stowage opening immediately to the working deck containing the life-raft(s) only.

B.   For yachts built after 1.7.83
         Life-raft(s) may only be stowed under the working deck provided:
         (a) the stowage compartment is watertight or self draining.
         (b) if the stowage compartment is not watertight, then the floor of the special stowage is defined as the cockpit sole for the purposes of rule 6.23.2
         (c) the cover of this compartment shall be capable of being opened under water pressure.

C.   Life-raft(s) packed in a valise and not exceeding 40kg may be securely stowed below deck adjacent to the companionway.

D. Each raft shall be capable of being got to the lifelines within 15 seconds.

E. Must be designed and used solely for saving life at sea.

F. Must have at least two separate buoyancy compartments, each of which must be automatically inflatable; each raft must be capable of carrying its rated capacity with one compartment deflated.

G. Must have a canopy to cover the occupants.

H. Must have a valid annual certificate from the manufacturer or an approved servicing agent certifying that it has been inspected, that it complies with the above requirements and stating the official capacity of the raft which shall not be exceeded. The certificate, or a copy thereof, to be carried on board the yacht.

I. Must have the following equipment appropriately secured to each raft:

    Sea anchor or drogue
1 Bellows, pump or other means for maintaining inflation of air chambers
1 Signalling light
3 Hand flares
1 Bailer
1 Repair Kit
2 Paddles
1 Knife

11.42 Provision for emergency water and rations to accompany raft.

11.51 *Life ring(s)*, at least one horseshoe-type life-ring equipped with a waterproof light and drogue within reach of the helmsman and ready for instant use.

11.52 At least one horseshoe-type life-ring equipped with a drogue and a self-igniting light having a duration of at least 45 minutes within reach of the helmsman and ready for instant use.

11.53 At least one more horseshoe-type life-ring equipped with a whistle, dye marker, drogue, a self-igniting high-intensity water light, and a pole and flag. The pole shall be permanently extended and attached to the ring with 25 ft. (8m) of floating line and is to be of a length and so ballasted that the flag will fly at least 6ft. (1.8m) off the water.

11.61 *Distress signals* to be stowed in waterproof container(s), and meeting the following requirements for each category, as indicated:

11.62   Twelve red parachute flares.

11.63   Four red parachute flares.

11.64   Four red hand flares.

11.65   Four white hand flres.

11.66   Two orange smoke day signals.

11.7 *Heaving line* (50 ft. [16m] minimum length) readily accessible to cockpit.

Reprinted by permission, Offshore Racing Council, from "Special Equipment Regulations," 1983.

2. Rules

.3 The Offshore Racing Council Special Regulations Governing Minimum Equipment and Accommodations Standards, Category 2 with the following additions and changes.

11.41 Life raft(s) need not have a canopy.

(a) Life rafts must be accompanied by a certificate of inspection and compliance by an inspection station approved by the Federal Aviation Agency, U.S. Coast Guard, the manufacturer or other authority dated within twelve months of the first race.

It is the skipper's responsibility to be familiar with these regulations, to assure compliance and to use equipment approved by his national authority when required.

.4 The International Rules for the Prevention of Collisions at Sea.

Special SORC Racing Instructions

3. Eligibility

.1 To be eligible a yacht must be a single-hulled, self-righting enclosed-cabin sailing vessel with watertight self-bailing cockpit conforming with the ORC Special Regulations Governing Minimum Equipment and Accommodations. . . .

5. Owner's and Skipper's Responsibilities

.1 The term "Skipper" as used in these Conditions and Sailing Instructions shall mean the person whether or not the owner of the yacht who is designated on the entry form as "Skipper" and who is in charge of the yacht.

.3 The safety of the yacht and its crew is the sole and inescapable responsibility of the Skipper who must ensure that the yacht is fully found, thoroughly seaworthy and manned by an experienced crew who are physically fit. The Skipper of the yacht must be satisfied as to the soundness of the hull, spars, rigging and all gear. He must ensure that all equipment is properly maintained and stowed and that he and the crew know where it is kept and how it is to be used.

.4 Neither the establishment of equipment regulations nor any inspection of a yacht in any way limits or reduces the complete and unlimited responsibility of a yacht's Skipper.

7. Crew

.1 The minimum crew shall be four persons in addition to the Skipper.

.3 A complete and accurate list of names and addresses of all the crew members for each race of the series must be filed with the race committee prior to the first race in which any yacht competes. Subsequent crew changes should be delivered to the SORC Executive Secretary.

9. Other Regulations

.1   Yachts must have suitable inboard auxiliary propulsion power and adequate fuel on board for running at least 75 nautical miles under power. . . .

.2   . . . All yachts shall monitor the distress frequency upon sighting any distress signal either day or night.

.3   Man overboard poles and radio antennae extending beyond the perimeter of the yacht shall not be considered as part of the yacht and equipment. . . .

10. Rule Compliance

.2   All yachts shall submit a Certification of Inspection indicating compliance with the Special Regulations Governing Minimum Equipment and Accommodations Standards, Category 2 as modified herein to the SORC Executive Secretary before racing. Such Certification of Inspection shall not be construed as certification of seaworthiness of any yacht nor shall the SORC or its inspectors be liable for the safety of a yacht, its equipment, or its crew.

17. Retiring and Abandoning

.1   A yacht which does not start or which retires from a race should wear her ensign and keep well clear of yachts racing. The Skipper shall, at the earliest possible opportunity, notify the Race Committee and the USCG of this fact. Failure to give such notification will result in disqualification and, at the discretion of the SORC, rejection of entries for future races.

Reprinted by permission, Southern Ocean Racing Conference, Inc., from "Conditions and Sailing Instructions," 1982.

HYPOTHERMIA

What Is It?

A condition in which exposure to cold air and/or water lowers body core temperature. Death can result from too low a brain and heart temperature.

Why Be Concerned?

Hypothermia, even mild cases, decreases crew efficiency and increases risk of costly accidents. Smart planning against hypothermia can give a winning competitive edge. Be a WARM WINNER, not a COOL LOSER.

Prevention

- Wear warm clothing and a PFD (Personal Flotation Device). Have survival suits available for crew. Insulate all areas of the body, especially the high heat-loss areas: head, neck, armpits, sides of chest, and groin. Keep warm and dry, but avoid sweating; wear layered clothes.

- Rotate watch frequently.

- Get plenty of rest, prevent fatigue.

- Drink hot soup and sweet drinks for energy; *no* alcohol.

- Prevent dehydration; watch urine color (drink more if color becomes more intense).

- Avoid seasickness.

- Consider special medical problems of crew members.

- Have proper below-deck accommodations for cold and rough weather.

- Require that two or more of the crew be trained in CPR (cardiopulmonary resuscitation).

APPENDIX C

Recognizing and Treating Hypothermia

H.E.L.P.
(Heat Escape Lessening Posture)

- *Head out of water, including back of head*

- *Arms against sides, chest and PFD*

- *Lower legs crossed, knees raised as much as waves and stability permit, but keep knees together*

HUDDLE Two or more crew holding together

- *Heads out of water, including backs of heads*

- *Arms hugging each other over PFDs*

- *Maximum body contact, especially at chest, reducing heat loss*

- *Legs intertwined as much as possible*

- *Talk to maintain morale*

REMEMBER:
NO ONE IS A SURVIVOR UN-TIL RESCUED. KEEP CALM. MAKE YOURSELF VISIBLE.

- Have low-temperature rectal thermometer in first-aid kit.

Survival

- **If boat is in trouble,** get into survival suits or float coats. Radio for help: give position, number of crew, injuries, boat description. Make visual distress signals. Keep survival suits on until trouble ends. Stay below if possible. Remain aboard until sinking inevitable.

- **If going overboard,** launch life raft and EPIRB (Emergency Position Indicating Radio Beacon). Take visual distress signals with you. Get into raft, stay out of water. Remain near boat.

- **If in the water,** crew should stay together near boat. This makes everyone easier to find, and helps morale. Enter life raft, keep survival suit on.

- **If not wearing survival suits,** keep clothes and boots on for some insulation and flotation. Keep hat on to protect head. Get all or as much of body out of water as soon as possible—into raft, swamped boat, flotsam. Avoid swimming and treading water, which increase heat loss. **Minimize exposed body surface:** use H.E.L.P. and HUDDLE positions when possible.

RANGES OF HYPOTHERMIA SYMPTOMS

Note: Most physical symptoms vary with each individual and may be unreliable indicators of core body temperature. Only a low-temperature rectal thermometer gives reliable core temperature (the mouth cools too rapidly). In general, as body temperature falls, symptoms will increase.

MILD CONDITION (36-34°C, 97-93°F)
- Shivering, cold hands and feet

- Still alert and able to help self

- Numbness in limbs, loss of dexterity, clumsiness

- Pain from cold

MODERATE CONDITION (34-32°C, 93-90°F)
- Shivering may decrease or stop

SEVERE CONDITION (32-28°C, 90-82°F)
- Shivering decreases or stops

- Loss of reasoning and recall, confusion, abnormal behavior

- Victim appears drunk; very clumsy, slurs speech, denies problem and may resist help

- Victim semiconscious to unconscious

- Muscular rigidity increasing

CRITICAL CONDITION (28°C, 82°F and below)
- *Unconscious,* may appear dead

- Little or no apparent breathing

- Pulse slow and weak, or no pulse found

- Skin cold, may be bluish-gray color

- Eyes may be dilated

- Very rigid

HYPOTHERMIA FIRST AID

All Cases
- Apply mild heat (comfortable to your elbow) to head, neck, chest and groin—use hot water bottles, warm moist towels

- Move victim to dry shelter and warmth

- Handle gently

- Remove wet clothes—cut off if necessary

- Cover with blankets or sleeping bag; insulate from cold—keep head and neck covered

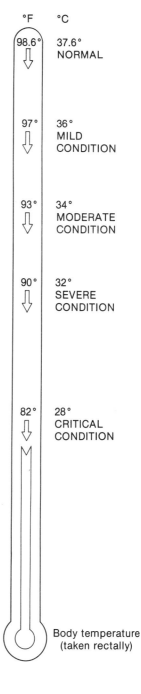

Body temperature (taken rectally)

°F   °C

98.6° 37.6°
       NORMAL

97°   36°
       MILD
       CONDITION

93°   34°
       MODERATE
       CONDITION

90°   32°
       SEVERE
       CONDITION

82°   28°
       CRITICAL
       CONDITION

Mild Cases

- Primary task is to prevent further heat loss and allow body to rewarm itself
- Give warm, sweet drinks—*no* alcohol
- Apply gentle heat source to stabilize temperature
- Exercise to generate heat
- Keep victim warm for several hours

Moderate Cases

- Same as above
- Limit exercise
- Offer sips of warm, sweet liquids only after victim is *fully conscious,* begins to rewarm, and is able to swallow
- Have victim checked by doctor

Severe Cases

- Obtain medical advice as soon as possible using your radio
- Assist victim, but avoid jarring him—rough handling may cause cardiac arrest or ventricular fibrillation of heart
- No food or drink
- Ignore pleas of "Leave me alone, I'm O.K." *Victim is in serious trouble*—keep continuous watch over victim
- Treat as for shock—lay down in bunk, wedge in place, elevate feet, keep immobile
- Apply external mild heat to head, neck, chest, and groin—keep temperature from dropping, but avoid too rapid a temperature rise
- Transport soon, gently, to hospital

Critical

- *Always assume patient is revivable—don't give up*

- Handle with *extreme care*

- Tilt the head back to open the airway—look, listen, and feel for breathing and pulse for *one to two full minutes*

- If there is any breathing or pulse, no matter how faint or slow, *do not give CPR,* but keep close watch on vital sign changes

- Stabilize temperature with external heat sources; also use naked chest-to-back warming by other crew member (leave legs alone), and/or use rescuer's warm breath exhaled in victim's face and in unison with his breathing

- If no breathing or no pulse for one to two full minutes, *begin CPR immediately*

- *Medical help imperative—hospitalization needed*

Warning

- First aid for severe and critical hypothermia is to add heat to stabilize temperature only. Rapid rewarming may be fatal; it will, at least, cause complications. Allow body to rewarm itself slowly.

- Body core temperature lags behind skin temperature during rewarming. Keep victim protected for extended period after apparent full recovery or medical help arrives. Many hours, even days, are required for return to normal temperature. Avoid reexposure to cold.

- Always assume hypothermia is present in all man-overboards.

- In a helicopter rescue, protect victim—especially the head—from rotor blast wind chill.

Reprinted by permission, United States Yacht Racing Union, 1982

Bibliography

Baker, Bob, "Storm Avoidance for Hire," *Motor Boating & Sailing*, May 1980.

Barrett, Peter, "Carte Blanche," *Yacht Racing/Cruising*, September 1980.

Barton, Robert, "Personal Performance, Safety and Comfort," *Yacht Racing/Cruising*, July/August 1979.

———"Upwind in Heavy Air," *Yacht Racing/Cruising*, October 1980.

Benjamin, Steve, "The Right Clothes for Racing," *Yachting*, December 1979.

———"Setting Up for Heavy Air Beats," *Sail*, June 1979.

Bouzaid, Chris, "Going to Windward in Heavy Weather," *Sail*, February 1979.

Bower, Carolyn, "A Watch System That Works," *Cruising World*, December 1979.

Brogdon, Bill, "Waves—They Mean What They Say," *Motor Boating & Sailing*, December 1979.

Bruce, Eroll, *Deep Sea Sailing*, McKay, 1979.

Budlong, John, "Managing a Boat in Heavy Weather," *Sail*, September 1979.

Bunker, Capt. Moss, "A Sea of Horrors," *The Ensign*, December 1980.

Chapman, Charles F., and Elbert S. Maloney, *Piloting, Seamanship & Small Boat Handling*, 55th ed, Hearst Marine Books, 1981.

Clemens, John, "What Now, Skipper?," *Yachting*, December 1979.

Cohen, Michael M., M.D., "Seasickness," *Yachting*, December 1979.

Coles, K. Adlard, *Heavy Weather Sailing*, John De Graff, Inc., 1981.

Colgate, Steve, *Fundamentals of Sailing, Cruising, and Racing*, W. W. Norton, 1978.

———"Taking Control Downwind," *Sail*, May 1980.

Dowty, Karen Jones, "Reassessing the Survival Situation," *Sail*, January 1980.

Gross, Tom, "When Rescue Is a Necessity," *Sail*, January 1980.

Hammond, Jeff, "You Bet Your Life," *Motor Boating & Sailing*, May 1979.

Jobson, Gary, *How to Sail*, Ziff-Davis, 1980.

———*USYRU Sailing Instructor's Manual*, 2nd Ed, 1981.

———*The Yachtsman's Pocket Almanac*, Simon & Schuster, 1981.

———and Ted Turner, *The Racing Edge*, Simon & Schuster, 1979.

Kirschenbaum, Jerry, "Help From Above," *Sail*, October 1980.

Knights, Jack, "The Storm Force Fastnet," *Sail*, October 1979.

Lane, Carl, *The Boatman's Manual*, W. W. Norton, 1979.

Marshall, Roger, "Upgrading Helmsmanship," *Sail*, February 1980.

———"Getting Ready for the Rough Stuff," *Sail*, October 1980.

Mellor, John, "Techniques for Towing," *Sail*, February 1980.

Nye, Richard, "Lessons from the Fastnet Disaster," *Yachting*, March 1980.

Oakes, Rod, "Performance Cruising," *Yacht Racing/Cruising*, March 1980.

O'Boyle, Bonnie, "Life Jackets That Can Let You Down," *Motor Boating & Sailing*, July 1979.

Payne, Robert, "Surviving Hurricane Assault," *Sail*, February 1981.

Perry, Dave, "Heavy Weather Slalom," *Yacht Racing/Cruising*, October 1980.

Richardson, Kent, "Saved by an EPIRB," *Yachting*, July 1979.

Roth, Hal, *After 50,000 Miles*, W. W. Norton, 1977.

Rousmaniere, John, *Fastnet Force 10*, W. W. Norton, 1980.

Staff, "Fastnet: Harsh Lessons," *Sail*, February 1980.

Staff, "From the Experts—The Thistle," from "Thistle Tuning" column in *Yacht Racing/Cruising*, February 1980.

Stephens, Rod, "Man Overboard," *Sail*, June 1979.

———"Ready for Heavy Weather Sailing," *Yachting*, April 1980.

Street, Don, "Battening Down," *Sail*, February 1980.

———"Handling Force 9," *Motor Boating & Sailing*, July 1979.

Taylor, Steve, "Anatomy of a Capsize," *Yacht Racing/Cruising*, September 1980.

Watts, Alan, "Contrails Can Improve Forecasts," *Sail*, April 1979.

———"Understanding Your Barometer," *Sail*, November 1979.

"What Speed Can Wind Really Have?," *Sail*, February 1981.

List of Diagrams

Index